MEN VERSUS THE MAN

MEN versus the MAN

Henry Louis
MENCKEN

Robert Rives
LA MONT

preface by John
DERBYSHIRE

UNDERWORLD AMUSEMENTS

This edition by Underworld Amusements, 2011
www.underworldamusements.com

Foreword by John Derbyshire, ©2011
Cover illustration by Josh Latta, ©2011
Design & editing by Kevin I. Slaughter

Print
ISBN 978-0-9830314-2-0
eBook
ISBN 978-0-9830314-4-4

CONTENTS

PREFACE
Men versus the Man, 100 Years On

Preamble

Let me do a little scene-setting here. It is March of 1910—just 100 years and change ago. William Howard Taft is in the White House; Edward the Seventh, very nearly Taft's equal in girth, was on the British throne. China's last Emperor was in the Forbidden City, and the Russian Empress was under the spell of Rasputin.

Mark Twain and Leo Tolstoy were still alive. The population of the U.S.A. was 92 million, including 450,000 veterans of the Civil War (North and South) and 162 households recorded in the census of that year as "living in polygamy." Thirteen percent of us were foreign born. Total government spending was eight percent of GDP.

The automobile was settling in, airplanes were still a novelty, Picasso was painting, Mahler was composing, Nijinsky was dancing, Caruso was singing, H.G. Wells was writing, and Mary Pickford had just started in the movies. The year's hit pop song was "Let Me Call You Sweetheart."

Adolf Hitler was living in a homeless shelter in Vienna, Lenin was writing angry pamphlets in cheap rooming houses, Stalin was on the run from the Tsar's secret police, FDR was a lawyer on Wall Street, Churchill was Trade Secretary in H.H. Asquith's cabinet, Gandhi was agitating for civil rights in South Africa, and Mao Tse-Tung was in high school. Barry Goldwater was in diapers and Ronald Reagan was a twinkle in his Dad's eye.

There was a lot of 20th century still to run.

MEN VERSUS THE MAN

H.L. Mencken was 29 years old, in his fourth year at the *Baltimore Sun*. He'd been a reporter and drama critic for the *Baltimore Herald*, which went belly-up in 1906. He'd also contributed some light, jokey pieces to the *Herald*: not quite opinion columns in the modern sense, but that was because Mencken had not yet *invented* the modern newspaper opinion column. He'd published a book of verse, a book about Shaw's plays, and a study of Nietzsche.

In March of this year, 1910, he published another book, *Men versus the Man*. Terry Teachout, in his 2002 biography of Mencken, gives the book the merest passing mention, thus:

> He... conducted an epistolary debate on individualism with a socialist acquaintance that eventually appeared in book form as *Men versus the Man*... (it) shows how his political thinking had solidified—hardened, really. The law of the survival of the fittest, he declares, is "immutable," thus making socialism an absurdity; human progress is the product of the will to power, and all social arrangements failing to take this fact into account are doomed to failure; inequality is natural, even desirable, both in and of itself and as an alternative to mob rule; the world exists to be run by "the first-caste man."

That's not a bad summary. I am, however, a lazy and inattentive reader, and had forgotten all about *Men versus the Man* probably even before I set down Teachout's biography.

Then in early September this year an occasional e-correspondent of mine sent me an email with some comments on, quote from him, "a fun book that I hadn't heard of before." It was that same book, *Men versus the Man*.

These comments piqued my curiosity more than Teachout's had. Off I went to the second-hand book websites, and there it was. It cost me $21.85, much more than I'd normally spend on a book. If I want a new book, I cadge a copy from a literary editor or from the author: if I want an old book I log on to Abebooks.com, and consider myself cheated if I pay more for the book than for the postage. With Mencken though you can be sure of a decent intellectual return on investment.

Well, what's it all about? As Teachout says, the book is laid out in the form of an epistolary debate. There are twelve letters altogether, around twenty pages per, six from Mencken's socialist friend and six responses from Mencken himself.

The friend is Robert Rives La Monte. An entire hour of internet browsing turned up nothing about this gentleman other than that he was the author of a handful of books and pamphlets on socialism in the early 20th century. (I shall quote from another one of them in a little while.) In desperation I even tried using his name as a search argument in Google Images: it's surprising how often you can find nothing written about a person, and yet turn up a picture. Google Images did offer some rather pleasing erotic paintings by an obscure French artist utterly unrelated to my quarry, but nothing else.

Mencken, in a remark I'll quote at the end of this preface, speaks of La Monte in passing as living on a country estate, so perhaps he was an early specimen of the limousine liberal; but Mencken is not very reliable on matters relating to people he disagreed with, so we cannot say for sure.

La Monte therefore remains a shadowy figure to me, and so must to you. The important thing about him for our purposes here tonight is that in 1907 he had published a book preaching socialism; Mencken must have read it; the two of them engaged in these six exchanges in 1909; and the following year they put them out in book form.

PLUS ÇA CHANGE...

So here we have six letters from La Monte, a Marxist socialist, and six letters in response from H.L. Mencken, a Nietzschean individualist, the correspondence conducted 101 years ago.

The intellectual fun of reading material like this is in sorting out what, after the lapse of a century, has changed, and what has stayed the same.

The thing that has most obviously changed is socialism. La Monte is preaching the old-time religion of unmodified Marxism, with its iron-clad faith in modes of production as being prior to every aspect of human nature and human history.

Everything about human society—everything we should nowadays call "the culture": law, religion, ethics, customs, science, literature, crime, the family, the nation—is mere superstructure, built on the foundation rocks of property relations. Quote from La Monte:

> So long as science was a mere shuttlecock tossed hither and thither by varying class interests nothing worthy of the name of science was so much as possible. Not until the Social Revolution shall have wiped out class lines forever, will a true science, that is a broadly human, instead of a class, science, arise. [1]

Or again:

> Here, we Socialists have the advantage of you, for we do know, in the language of Friedrich Nietzsche, "how ideals are manufactured on earth." We do know that human ideals are determined by the modes of production and exchange; and, therefore, we know that the commercial ideal of boundless wealth will persist just as long as the means of production and distribution remain private property, and we do know that the Social Revolution, now close at hand, which will transform these into common or collective property will usher in the new and glorious ideal of social service... [2]

If you change the economic fundamentals, therefore, you

---

[1]   p. 131

[2]   p. 177

will transform society, and liberate human nature to flourish in freedom, fulfilling the potential it always had, and always has, in every one of us.

The working people of the industrial world of course know this. How can you be oppressed and not know it? They are gathering in strength, and will soon come into their birthright.

It all sounds preposterously naïve to us now, a hundred years later. The naïvety of it in fact became apparent to socialists rather soon. The disillusioning event was World War One, when the workers of the industrial world, instead of responding to the crisis by casting down the mighty from their thrones and exalting the meek and humble, obediently, and in fact enthusiastically, marched off to war under their upper-class officers, singing patriotic songs.

World War One was a terrible shock to socialists. La Monte himself recorded the shock in a book he wrote in 1917, title *The Socialist Attitude on the War*:

> Most of us have realized at least subconsciously, that we were at heart dreamers...The choicest product of our uncurbed imaginations was a kind of Marxian Economic Man, a sort of... marionette without red blood or emotional impulses, who responded solely to economic stimuli. Just show this curious monster where lay his economic interest... and he could be depended on to pursue it ruthlessly... Since August 4th, 1914 even the dullest of us are beginning to realize that men and women of flesh and blood do not act like economic marionettes.

That belongs to what my friend Roger Kimball calls "the literature of disabusement." It was obvious that Marx had not gotten things quite right.

Through the 1920s all sorts of awkward questions were tackled by theorists like George Lukács and Antonio Gramsci. Was Marx right in his methods but wrong in his data? If all non-economic facts were part of the secondary, transformable superstructure, then wasn't Marxism itself part of that superstructure too? Most of all: If the consciousness of the working classes was formed by their economic condition at the bottom of capitalist society, why had they so eagerly marched off to fight for their bourgeois masters?

Much brainpower was devoted through the 1920s and 1930s to working out satisfactory answers to these kinds of questions — answers that would leave intact the essential Marxist critique of capitalist society and the even more essential (one cannot help thinking) dream of a New Jerusalem populated by New Men.

Obviously some sort of feedback loop was present and had somehow been missed by Marx. The culture of bourgeois society might be a flimsy and malleable "superstructure," but once in place it worked on the minds of the proletariat somehow, giving them "false consciousness," a notion already found in an embryonic form in the works of Engels. Instead of being a marionette who, once his economic interest had been pointed out to him, "could be depended on to pursue it ruthlessly," the proletarian became, in the Western Marxism that developed through the middle decades of the 20th century, a *dumb* marionette helplessly lost in illusions foisted on him by bourgeois culture.

Since Johnny Prole wasn't capable of bringing forth the New Jerusalem in this sedated condition, some surrogate proletariat had to be found. It accordingly was, in groups so marginalized and oppressed that they, or at least useful numbers of them, were immune to false consciousness: women, blacks, homosexuals, Muslims, and so on. Recruitment into these legions of the oppressed continues to the present day, with "immigrants" the most recently enlisted. Speaking personally, as an immigrant myself, I find this baffling; but no doubt I am suffering from false consciousness.

There has thus been a great change in the nature of socialism since 1910. From the naïve romanticism of La Monte, via the great disillusioning of World War One, to the reconstructive efforts of Lukács and Gramsci in the 1920s, the labors of the Frankfurt school through the thirties and forties, to the sixties New Left and the Political Correctness, romantic xenophilia, and deference to transgressive sexuality of our own time, it's been a long hundred years for socialists.

*   *   *

What of Mencken's ideas? They belong more to a *tendency*, an outlook, than to a systematized school of thought like Marxism; but is that tendency still with us? If so, has it undergone any modification since 1910?

Well, plainly the broad tendency Mencken represented is still with us, or else why would we be assembled here under his name? And yes, its actual expression has undergone some changes this past hundred years, though I think in scope and scale nothing like those that have been forced upon socialists by the repeated muggings they have suffered at the hands of reality. Being rooted at least approximately in reality, Mencken's ideas have been more robust, much better able to take care of themselves.

But modification, yes. The most obvious change has been in our thinking about the relations between biology and human society. The modern phase of that thinking had been fired off by the publication of Darwin's *On the Origin of Species* fifty years before the Mencken-La Monte exchanges.

Just dwell on that span of time for a moment. Fifty years separates us from 1960, so that Mencken was to Darwin's theory of evolution by natural selection approximately as we are to the first stirrings of the sociobiology revolution in the human sciences, taking that revolution as having begun with William Hamilton's papers in 1964.

The rediscovery of Mendel's work on inherited characteristics was, for Mencken and La Monte, in the very recent past, too recent for them to have assimilated it. Mencken doesn't mention

Mendel at all in this book, and La Monte only mentions him to betray the fact that he completely misunderstands Mendel's discoveries. The actual biochemical mechanisms of inheritance were of course completely mysterious to both writers, the discovery of DNA 40-odd years in the future.

In these kinds of circumstances, and among people like Mencken and La Monte, neither of whom had any real scientific training,[3] scientific ideas tend to get misappropriated for emotional, polemical, or political purposes. In Mencken's case this most conspicuously happened with the collection of ideas that later came to be called "social Darwinism."

Herbert Spencer is the villain here. If there is a prize awarded in Hell for the coining of phrases that lead men into gross error, Spencer must be the winner in the nineteenth century division for having given us the phrase "survival of the fittest." The subtle and fruitful notion of Darwinian fitness, which you actually need a lot of math to appreciate in all its elegance and explanatory power, got dragged over into economics and politics and was soon synonymous with robber barons and Nietzschean blonde beasts. (That latter, by the way, a confusion which would have infuriated Nietzsche, who actually understood Darwin quite well.)

Mencken was a social Darwinist in this regrettable sense, and freely deployed the phrase "survival of the fittest" in defense of his social ideas. Nobody would do that nowadays.

Unfortunately this is not because, or only very partially because, proper understanding of biology is now more widespread. It is much more an aspect of what my friend Peter Brimelow calls "Hitler's revenge." We defeated the Nazi armies and killed their ideology; but the horrors that ideology had generated left us terrified that it might rise from the dead. To prevent that happen-

---

3   A fact known in Mencken's case. In the case of La Monte, it can be inferred, at a very high confidence level, from his contributions to *Men versus the Man*.

ing, we ruled out of polite discourse all the intellectual streams that had fed into the Nazi pond, of which social Darwinism was certainly one.

That we might be throwing out some babies with the bathwater was not considered. That the ideas of social Darwinism—however wrong-headed the implication that they had something to do with *actual* Darwinism—that those ideas might have some merit, was no longer a thinkable thought.

The Trotskyists of my college days, defending Marxism against the charge that it inevitably led to tyranny and mass murder under despots like Stalin, Mao, and Castro, used to chide us that "an idea should not be held responsible for the people who hold it." That Hitler was, as he undoubtedly was, a variety of social Darwinist, killed off social Darwinism stone dead. Somehow the fact that Stalin was, as he undoubtedly was, a variety of socialist, did not kill off socialism. These are the paradoxes of intellectual history.

To show how sensibilities have changed, here is Mencken writing in a way nobody, not even Mencken's greatest fan, would write nowadays.

> As a matter of fact, the typical low-caste man is entirely unable to acquire that power of ordered and independent reasoning which distinguishes the man of higher caste. You may, by dint of heroic endeavors, instil into him a parrotlike knowledge of certain elemental facts, and he may even make a shift to be a schoolmaster himself, but he will remain a stupid and ignorant man, none the less. More likely, you will find that he is utterly unable to assimilate even the simplest concepts. The binomial theorem is as far beyond his comprehension as an epigram in Persian. And this inability to understand the concepts formulated by others is commonly but the symptom of a more marked incapacity for formulating new concepts of his own. In the true sense, such a being cannot think.

Robert Rives La Monte & H. L. Mencken

Within well-defined limits, he may be trained, just as any other sentient creature my be trained, but beyond that he cannot go.

The public school can never hope to raise him out of his caste. It can fill him to the brim—but then it must stop. He is congenitally unteachable. A year after he has left school, he has forgotten nearly all that he learnt there. At twenty-one, when the republic formally takes him into its councils, he is laboring with pick and shovel in his predestined ditch, a glad glow in his heart and a strap around his wrist to keep off rheumatism.[4]

We're some distance there from No Child Left Behind.

This is not even to mention Mencken's opinions of, for instance, the "foul, ignorant, thieving, superstitious, self-appointed negro preacher of the Black Belt, whose mental life is made up of three ambitions—to eat a whole hog at one meal, to be a white man in heaven, and to meet a white woman, some day, in a lonely wood."[5]

...PLUS C'EST LA MÊME CHOSE

So much for what has changed this hundred years. What, on the evidence of *Men versus the Man*, has stayed the same?

The short answer is: underlying notions. Human thinking about human nature and human society has only a small number of modes, most of which first showed up among the ancients. The actual expression of any mode is to some degree a creature of time and fashion, but the fundamentals really don't vary.

The most fundamental of the fundamentals in La Monte's case is the faith he expresses, using the language of original unmodified Marxism, in innate human equality. To be sure, he says, we observe much inequality, both in men's conditions and in

---

4   p. 141-142

5   p. 194

their capabilities; but those observed inequalities are distortions brought about by an unjust social order.

That was by no means a nonsensical opinion in 1910. My own mother, just sixteen years later, though an intelligent and bookish child, had to leave school at age fourteen and go into domestic service. Mum was one of 13 children of a coal-miner, and her family needed her to generate some income. Many a talent was stunted by social deprivation in Mencken's time, though I believe this was less true in the United States than in England, or perhaps anywhere.[6]

It does not follow that every coal miner's daughter was a stifled genius. That was the implication taken by the socialists, though. Human nature, they believed, has no structure, human capabilities have no relation to biology. Released from the constraints of late-capitalist society, the human spirit would blossom—not merely in general, but in every single particular human being. Every person would be a Shakespeare, a Mozart, a Faraday... though it was left unclear which one he would decide to be: perhaps all, either in series or in parallel.

This conception has survived all the intellectual storms endured by 20th-century socialism, all those muggings by reality. It's on display at a theater near you right now, in the movie Waiting for Superman. Here I bring forward my favorite quotation on this subject. It is *New York Times* reporter Deborah Solomon, interviewing Charles Murray two years ago on the publication of Charles' book *Real Education*. Quote from Ms. Solomon: "Given the opportunity, most people could do most anything."

---

6   The stunting, though no doubt there were real and tragic cases, should not be exaggerated. In free societies, even in the 1920s, it was hard to keep a good man down. Or woman: After that couple of years at Atherstone Hall, my mother thought "The hell with this!" and got herself a career in nursing. When she retired in 1972, she was second in command of the nursing staff at a large hospital.

La Monte agrees.

Socialism will abolish poverty and satiety, and make joyousness the dominant note of humanity; it will make it impossible for self-interest to clash with social welfare, and will thus make the Golden Rule work universally and automatically. "May we not expect," asks Kautsky, "that under such conditions a new type of mankind will arise which will be far superior to the highest type which culture has hitherto created? An Over-man (Über-mensch), if you will, not as an exception but as a rule, an Over-man compared with his predecessors, but not as opposed to his comrades, a noble man who seeks his satisfaction not by being great among crippled dwarfs, but great among the great, happy among the happy—who does not draw his feeling of strength from the fact that he raises himself upon the bodies of the down-trodden, but because a union with his fellow-workers gives him courage to dare the attainment of the highest tasks."[7]

This faith in the infinite malleability of the individual human being has survived all these decades unscathed, from the Taft presidency to Obama's, from Mary Pickford to Miley Cyrus. And of course it long predates La Monte. In the form of the *tabula rasa* concept, it goes all the way back through intellectual history to Avicenna and Aristotle.

It was socialists who carried it forward through the 20th century though, and made it into an obscurantist hindrance to our understanding of ourselves. E.O. Wilson pointed this out in his 1978 book *On Human Nature*:

The strongest opposition to the scientific study of human nature has come from a small number of Marxist biologists and anthropologists... They believe that nothing exists in the untrained human mind that cannot be readily channeled to the purposes of the revolutionary socialist state. When faced with the evidence

---

7   p. 186

of greater structure, their response has been to declare human nature off limits to further scientific investigation.

And if equality between individuals is a cherished principle, how much more equality between populations, however isolated and inbred. The socialist propagandist Stephen Jay Gould laid down the marker here, in a 1984 essay:

> Say it five times before breakfast tomorrow; more important, understand it as the center of a network of implication: "Human equality is a contingent fact of history."

Mencken is having none of that; and as today's race deniers, world-uplifters, educational romantics, and enthusiasts for unlimited immigration from absolutely everywhere all share their core assumptions with Robert Rives La Monte, however naïve his faith in the proletariat, *so* today's race realists, anti-globalists, educational reductionists, and immigration restrictionists can draw nourishment from Mencken, however coarse his disdain for what he unabashedly calls "the low-caste man."

Having introduced there Mencken's favorite term for the persons at the wrong end of his social Darwinism, I had better let him explain what he means by "caste." First, the "high-caste" man:

> What virtues do I demand in the man who claims enrollment in the highest caste? Briefly, I demand that he possess, to an unusual and striking degree, all of those qualities, or most of them, which most obviously distinguish the average man from the average baboon. If you look into the matter, you will find that the chief of these qualities is a sort of restless impatience with things as they are—a sort of insatiable desire to help along the evolutionary process. The man who possesses this quality is ceaselessly eager to increase and fortify his mastery of his environment. He has a vast curiosity and a vast passion for solving the problems it unfolds before him. His happiness lies in the consciousness that he has made some progress today in comprehending and turning to his

uses those forces which menaced him yesterday. His eye is fixed, not upon heaven, but upon earth; not upon eternity, but upon tomorrow. He enters the world infinitely superior to a mere brute... By his life and labors, the human race, or some part of it, makes some measurable progress, however small, upward from the ape.[8]

This is in contrast to the "low-caste" man, whom Mencken characterizes by "chronic and ineradicable suspiciousness, orthodoxy, stupidity, lack of foresight, and inability to learn."[9]

It is interesting that Mencken uses the word "caste" in this context. He was a writer who chose his words carefully, and it seems to me odd that he chose this one. The essence of caste is social separation and endogamy; yet Mencken makes it clear elsewhere that he favors social mobility.

Dealing thus with countless individuals, it sets them off, roughly, into castes, but there are no palpable barriers about these castes. A man born into the lowest may die in the highest. A race as generally inefficient as the African may produce an occasional Hannibal or Dumas,[10] and a race at the top of the scale may have its hordes of idiots. In one century, when the general environment of humanity puts a premium upon a certain kind of skill, the race best displaying it may rule the world, and two centuries later, when changes in environment make some other kind of skill more valuable, that same race may sink to practical slavery. The great reward is always

---

8   p. 107-108

9   p. 105

10   Mencken has confused geography with ethnography here. His entire experience of "Africans" was of African Americans, who are of sub-Saharan African ancestry, mixed to various degrees with white-European and Native American. Hannibal was Carthaginian, which is to say most likely a mix of Middle Eastern and Berber, most un-likely sub-Saharan African in any measure. Mencken is on firmer ground with Dumas *père*, though "African" is still a stretch: Dumas' paternal grandmother was a Haitian mulatto, but his other ancestors were all French. He was therefore at most one-eighth sub-Saharan African—about the same as Pushkin.

to the race, as to the individual, which best masters the present difficulty and meets the present need.[11]

This is a generous and broadminded view of social structure. While individuals have their particular inborn traits, and races their general ones, a person of great ability might rise from any kind of background, and there is no sign that Mencken would wish by any means to prevent that person's rise.

A socialist would say that we all have the same innate abilities in potential, but that those abilities wither and die under conditions of social oppression. You may not wish—Mencken plainly does not wish—to hold down any person from expressing his ability, but (says the socialist) the unjust society that you and Mencken so smugly accept will do the holding-down anyway. These are the same notions we see today in cant denunciations of "our failing schools" and the like.

While much has changed, therefore, much has stayed the same.

Will this argument ever end? There is some prospect that it might, possibly within our lifetimes... or some of our lifetimes. Information science, neurophysiology, molecular and computational genetics, population studies, and paleoanthropology are probing deeper and deeper into human nature. Some of the results have been over-sold and some of the difficulties—I think I'll say most of the difficulties—under-estimated, but there is visible progress in our understanding since technologies like brain imaging and gene sequencing came up this past twenty years.

The argument of *Men versus the Man* is one we are still having today. The content of the argument is the relative desirability of two approaches to our social life. On the one hand is proposed a society of *men*: a society in which none is allowed to rise too high above another, a society that subtracts great resources from

---

11   p. 197-198

the more able in an effort to raise up the less able. On the other hand is a society of *the man*: a society in which individuals are left to do what they can with their inherited capabilities, in conditions of maximum personal freedom and minimal state control.

The argument has been going on in one form or another for a couple of millennia. It is reasonable to hope that we might soon—in less than *another* century, I'd hope—attain sufficient understanding of our species to know beyond doubt which kind of society is more stable and enduring, which less likely to foster cruelty and injustice.

MENCKEN VERSUS *MEN VERSUS THE MAN*

Nine years later, which is to say in 1919, Mencken made a passing reference to *Men versus the Man*. This was in an essay on the Norwegian-American sociologist Thorstein Veblen, the man who gave us the phrase "conspicuous consumption." La Monte was quite taken with Veblen and had quoted him many times and at length in his sides of the exchanges with Mencken.

I'm going to leave you with Mencken's 1919 remarks as they make a nice coda to my preface:

> Back in the year 1909, being engaged in a bombastic discussion with what was then known as an intellectual Socialist (like the rest of the intelligentsia, he succumbed to the first fife-corps of World War I, pulled down the red flag, damned Marx as a German spy, and began whooping for Woodrow Wilson and Otto Kahn), I was greatly belabored and incommoded by his long quotations from a certain Prof. Thorstein Veblen, then quite unknown to me. My antagonist manifestly attached a great deal of importance to these borrowed sagacities, for he often heaved them at me in lengths of a column or two, and urged me to read every word of them. I tried hard enough, but found it impossible going. The more I read them, in fact, the less I could make of them, and so in the end, growing impatient and impolite, I denounced this Prof. Veblen as a geyser of pishposh, refused to waste any more

time upon his incomprehensible syllogisms, and applied myself to the other Socialist witnesses in the case, seeking to set fire to their shirts.

That old debate, which took place by mail (for the Socialist lived in levantine luxury on his country estate and I was a wage-slave attached to a city newspaper), was afterward embalmed in a dull book, and got the mild notice of a day. The book, by name, *Men versus the Man*, is now as completely forgotten as Baxter's *Saint's Rest* or the Constitution of the United States. I myself am perhaps the only man who remembers it at all, and the only thing I can recall of my opponent's argument (beyond the fact that it not only failed to convert me to Marxism, but left me a bitter and incurable scoffer at democracy in all its forms) is his curious respect for the aforesaid Veblen, and his delight in the learned gentleman's long, tortuous and (to me, at least) intolerably flapdoodlish phrases.

And today, ninety-one years further on, I am glad to preface this new edition of that book Mencken believed "completely forgotten"; and to have tried, at least, to illustrate that even so slight a production of our patron's mind, so long left to gather dust on the high back shelves of university libraries, might have something to tell us today.

JOHN DERBYSHIRE.

This preface is an expanded and revised form of an address given to the
H.L. Mencken Club, a dissident conservative group,
at the Club's annual meeting in Baltimore, October 22, 2010.

Robert Rives La Monte & H. L. Mencken

INTRODUCTION

THIS book is precisely what it pretends to be: a series of letters between friends. They were written because the general subject of the organization of society was one which vastly attracted both of us, and because a space of three hundred miles made a more intimate discussion impossible. Into them there went, not so much a learned review of the evidence and the prophets, as a record of personal, and often transient opinions and impressions. Changes of position are to be noticed in more than one place, but inasmuch as the purpose of each disputant was to shake the stand of the other, this proof of occasional success may be accepted, it is hoped, without impatience. It was thought best to print the letters without attempting to transform their epistolary freedom into a more sedate dialectic manner. They offer few new contributions of either fact or theory to the great questions they presume to discuss, but it is possible that they may be of some interest as showing how variously the accepted facts and theories appear and appeal to two somewhat eager inquirers.

LA MONTE.
MENCKEN.

LA MONTE'S FIRST LETTER

My Dear Mencken:

You and I are fairly typical of the hosts of educated young men and women of upper and middle class antecedents who are so far from satisfied with life as it is that the man in the street who styles us "knockers" does not come very wide of the mark. But yet we differ, and differ widely; you, in spite of your sturdy independence of mind, are in the main a disciple of Nietzsche, or, in other words, you are an Individualist whose ideal is a splendid aristocratic oligarchy of Beyond Men ruling over a hopelessly submerged rabble; I am a Socialist and a faithful disciple of Marx—not that I believe Marx to have been superhuman or infallible, but simply that I have found him to be right in so many cases, that I feel that there is a strong presumption that he is right even where I cannot clearly see that he is.

Let us first examine the grounds of our basic agreement, and then it will be easier to recognize the reason for the very wide divergence of our conclusions. We are both idealists in the sense that Don Quixote and Jesus Christ and Thomas Jefferson were idealists, but there are idealists and idealists. The difference depends upon the nature of the ideal. If the ideal be one capable of attainment or at least of reasonably close approximation, the idealist is what we call a practical man—he may even be a scientist, a materialist, or an atheist, as are many of the most effective and determined fighters for Socialism. If the ideal be one hopelessly beyond reach of attainment, if the idealist hitches his wagon to a star without having studied astronomy sufficiently to ascertain whether the orbit of the star is along a road over which his poor man-made wagon may pass in safety, then we call him a dreamer, a visionary, a Utopian, or a madman. It is probable that in our secret hearts this is the view each of us takes of the other.

You, recognizing that within historical times there has ever been a rabble of well-nigh sub-human men and women, believe that the only ideal that you, as a practical man, can accept is one including such a rabble. To you the man who proposes the abolition of this sub-human herd is a mystical dreamer who ignores the stern teachings of history. It must be admitted that much of the current Socialist literature—H. G. Wells' "New Worlds for Old," for instance—which presents Socialism as a scheme for human amelioration which Society is free to adopt or reject as it will, as a sort of patent panacea for human ills which the patient may or may not elect to imbibe; it must be admitted that the great bulk of this literature of polite propaganda goes far toward justifying your view.

But the typical Socialist of Germany, France, England, and America, the man or woman who gives his or her energies to educating and organizing and disciplining the wonderful, world-wide army, ever growing, ever marching forward, undismayed by defeat, sure of ultimate victory, already thirty million strong—the largest army under a single banner the world has ever seen—this typical, work-a-day, militant Socialist does not look upon himself or herself as a patent medicine vender, but as a John the Baptist proclaiming with no uncertain sound the advent of a New Order. Such an army inspired by a common faith, even though the faith be a delusion, animated by a common purpose, even though the purpose be incapable of realization, is a force that you as a practical man must reckon with.

But is the faith a delusion? Is the purpose incapable of realization? Let us see. If it is impossible for the Old Order to persist, then it follows that a New Order must come. I will postpone for the present discussing what that New Order is to be, and will proceed to show you that the Old Order *cannot* continue. I will give you as little history, political economy, and statistics as may be for two reasons; first, I know very little of such things myself; second, I wish to be agreeable to you, and I have found by experience that practical people have an extreme distaste for exact facts.

In a broad way the great difference between the economy of the Middle Ages and the economy of to-day, is that then production was chiefly for use—for local use—while to-day production is almost solely for sale. So that the smooth working of our modern industrial and commercial complexus depends upon the possibility of an adequate and uninterrupted sale of goods. Whenever the sale of goods is interrupted, as it was signally in 1873, 1893, and 1907, we have great panics.

Since the latter part of the eighteenth century we have had a continuous series of great mechanical inventions which have revolutionized and are day by day revolutionizing ever more rapidly our mode of production. The great net result of these changes is that the productive power of man has been hugely multiplied. I think I am well within the mark in saying that one hour's work to-day produces as much as one hundred hours' work in Adam Smith's day. Let us see what the concrete effect of this is. If we turn to the statistics gathered by our government at Washington, we find that in 1900 the average annual product per worker employed was in round numbers $2,000, while the average wages were about $400. The difficulty of disposing of the product is already beginning to appear. It is obvious that a man with $400 cannot purchase $2,000 worth of goods. Over fifty per cent. of our population actually belong to the working class. Add to them the farmers, whose purchasing power is not proportionally much greater, and you have all but a handful of our people. It is obvious that if our total product were composed of articles of personal consumption, and if we were limited to the home or domestic market, the disposition of the product *by sale* would be impossible. But we have foreign markets, and we produce pig-iron as well as pig-meat. The dependence of the first great manufacturing country, England, upon her foreign sales was recognized in her proud boast that England was the workshop of the world. But to-day in every market in the world England is meeting the ever-fiercer competition of Germany and America, while Japan is wresting the markets of the Orient from both Europe and America, and the coming industrial development of China—the true Yellow Peril—is already the nightmare of every far-seeing European and American conservative. The foreign market has been an immensely serviceable safety-valve, but inexorable economic development—or Fate or Kismet, if you will—is rapidly screwing it shut.

The other safety-valve—the application of capital and labor to the production of pig-iron instead of pig-meat—has been greatly developed in the past decade, and as a means of partial relief promises to outlast the foreign market safety-valve. The more capital and labor can be withdrawn from the production of articles of common everyday consumption, and employed in producing permanent industrial or transportation plant, the less becomes the *immediate* difficulty in disposing of our annual product. There can be no doubt that our recent period of prosperity was prolonged and the panic of 1907 postponed by the wholesale employment of capital and labor in such vast undertakings as the tunnels under the East and North rivers. But once such works are completed, they facilitate the production and distribution of goods, or save time or labor in some way, and thus in the long run accentuate the difficulty they temporarily relieve.

In our separate productive establishments a part of the capital employed must always be invested in permanent plant and a part paid out for wages day by day and week by week. Competition between rival plants has always compelled the constant improvement and development of machinery, and has thus compelled the owners constantly to invest larger and larger portions of their total capital in permanent plant. This change in what economists call the composition of capital has been forced upon the captains of industry irrespective of their wishes, and its effect has been to increase steadily and tremendously the disproportion between the value of the product and the purchasing-power of the wage-earners employed. Alike in the separate industrial plant and in the nation as a whole the constantly progressing change in the composition of capital—a change necessitated by the process itself and that must go on—in the long run makes ever more difficult the sale of the total product.

We are thus confronted by a condition, not a theory. The masses of the people are unable to purchase more than about one-fifth of the annual product, and this fatal lack of purchasing power is destined to increase steadily irrespective of any human will.

Are we not forced, my dear Mencken, to the conclusion that we are upon the threshold of economic changes so vast that no word short of Revolution is adequate to describe them? I sincerely believe that purely as a matter of economics the progressive and inexorable change in the technical composition of capital makes a Social Revolution inevitable, and further that this revolution is so close upon us that it behooves you and me, as prudent men, to prepare for it.

What sort of a revolution is it to be? Will it place in power an oligarchy of Nietzschean Immoralists—ancestors of the Beyond Men to-be? Something of this sort was predicted a few years ago by W. J. Ghent in his "Our Benevolent Feudalism," and has just been far more vividly described as a possibility by Jack London in that vigorous and brilliant, if depressing book, "The Iron Heel."

Or will it make the means of life the common possession of all, and thus abolish poverty forever, and usher in the era of fellowship so long foretold by bards and seers?

To answer these questions we must make a slight excursion into the field of psychology. Economics tell us that with all our male population between the ages of twenty-five and forty-five work ing three or four hours daily, we could produce enough to keep our whole population in such comfort as to-day requires an income of $5,000 a year.

If this is possible, and no statistician or economist is fool-hardy enough to deny it, whether or not the coming Social Revolution will bring it to pass depends upon the intelligence or desires of the masses. Let us see how these are determined. A man's mode of thought depends upon his mode of life. The man who depends largely upon changes in weather or climate, which seem to him to be utterly beyond the power of the human will to control, will be superstitious, whether he be a red Maori savage in New Zealand, or a barbarian tan-tinted grower of vegetables on Long Island or in Connecticut. But the man who works with machinery which runs with uniform regularity and is almost absolutely under human control and direction, ceases to be superstitious, reasons straight from cause to effect or from effect back to cause, ceases to go to church or chapel to pray to God for daily bread, and grows rudely and ominously unwilling to go barefooted because of an over-production of shoes, or hungry because of a plethora of beef and corn.

Now, as Professor Veblen has pointed out, the Machine Process is dominating directly and affecting indirectly ever more and more of our population, and the significant point is that these are just the people who suffer most from the continuance of the present system and who have everything to gain by making the factories and railroads and farms the common property of all the people. The factory worker is disciplined in co-operation in his daily work in the factory, he lives gregariously in tenements, and is accustomed to collective bargaining through the medium of his union. If he thinks at all, he must think toward Socialism. Often for years he hardly thinks at all, but panics come and bring unemployment. Unemployment is a powerful mental stimulus. When the panic passes and the unemployed man gets work, he is very likely to become a dues-paying member of the Socialist party.

Our argument has thus far brought us to the conclusion that a Social Revolution is imminent, and that the very conditions of their lives are compelling to socialistic thought and desires that ever growing host of the population employed in connection with machinery—the very part of the population who have nothing to fear from a revolution, who, in the words of Marx, "have nothing to lose but their chains, and a whole world to gain." But to-day no one wholly escapes the pervasive psychological effects of the Machine Process. Every twentieth century man and woman thinks more or less after the fashion of the factory worker of the nineteenth century. The thought-life of our time is day by day more and more affected by proletarian ideals and proletarian modes of ratiocination. Here and there individuals shielded by a favorable economic situation from direct contact with the hard facts of contemporary bread-winning are but little affected by the new tendencies, but no one wholly escapes this influence. Thus the economic and social forces which are organizing and drilling a mighty host of militant Socialists are at the same time making the rest of the population more or less mentally indisposed to combat with zeal and earnestness the forces making for a new social order.

Of the active components of our population the group which most nearly escapes the revolutionary psychological influences we have been considering, is the class of independent small producers and traders. But this class is fast disappearing before the advance of the trust and the department store. Where here and there we still find survivals of this formerly dominant typical American group, we find they have lost their sturdy independence of mind and character. They live in daily and hourly fear of economic extinction; they dread to open their daily papers lest they see in them that the manipulations of a Morgan or the enterprise of a Strauss shall have doomed them to bankruptcy. It is quite true that this little dying group is psychologically the bulwark of conservatism, but they are no longer a self-reliant militant group, and within a decade, as a social force or factor, they will be negligible.

The educated professional classes formerly could be relied on to think and write and speak in defense of the established order, but what of them to-day and to-morrow? The constant enlargement and growth of our facilities for higher education are overcrowding all the liberal professions, and are causing unemployment to be at least as common in professional life as it is in proletarian life. This difficulty is aggravated by the decreasing power of the middle classes to employ and support the professional men and women. Most of the ephemeral reform movements of the last two decades have been inspired and led by men"' of this class, but with the ever extending psychological influence of the Machine Process more and more of these discontented intellectuals will adopt the proletarian point of view, and place their trained minds at the disposal of the revolutionary forces.

We have surveyed very briefly the forces making for collectivism. What of the opposition? The number of those who have any real interest in opposing a Social Revolution is constantly growing, and must constantly grow, relatively smaller. But their political incompetence is even more striking than their numerical weakness. This surely needs no further illustration than a reference to the recent Congressional debates on railway rebate legislation and on the panic currency bill. The nearer the Social Revolution approaches, the smaller the body of its active opponents becomes, so that it seems likely that before the final struggle is begun the forces of reaction will number little more than the small group of the multi-millionaires and the cowardly slum-proletariat.

My conclusion, as you will have already seen, my dear Mencken, is that we are hard up against the Day of Judgment, and that the only issue possible is some form of collectivism or communism. Even if you and I felt that this outcome were deplorable, would it not be our duty, if we recognized its inevitability, to do our part toward preparing the public mind for the coming change? To oppose a change that we cannot prevent is but to dam up the mighty social forces and thus make violence and incendiarism and bloodshed the more likely. To work with the current of progress is to facilitate a peaceful revolution which will preserve for posterity unimpaired the priceless heritage we have received from the culture of the ages. In the words of Karl Marx, the Socialist is merely a sort of midwife helping the Old Order to give birth to the New with as little pain as may be.

But is the coming Social Revolution to be deplored? Is the present state of affairs so perfect that educated men such as you should give of their talent and energy to prolong it artificially? Is the socialistic ideal so abhorrent that it is to be postponed at any cost?

I feel that it is useless to quote to you from Robert Hunter's "Poverty" the dreadful statistics of the hosts who every year go to fill paupers' graves, or from H. G. Wells' "New Worlds for Old" the still more appalling statistics of the number of English school children who are underfed, diseased, and verminous. You would but repeat Nietzsche's commandment, "Be hard!" and say "These are the weak; let them go to the wall!" But surely even you would be unable to deafen your ears to "The Bitter Cry of the Children," so brilliantly made articulate by John Spargo. But I do confidently appeal to you in the name of aristocracy, of art, literature, and the drama. You believe that the aristocrats should rule because you deem them worthy to rule; you believe the mob should be abandoned to its lot because it is fit for nothing better. Go beneath the surface, my friend. To what do the aristocrats owe the noble and refined traits I freely admit and even rejoice that they possess? To the facts that they and their ancestors for several generations have had ample food and leisure. I do not say that a full stomach and time for idleness are all that is needed to make a gentleman or lady. But I do say that a gentleman or lady cannot be made without three generations of stomachs that have not suffered from innutrition, and three generations of hands that have not been so worn with toil as to make them unfitted for other occupations. The Socialist ideal would mean full stomachs and ample leisure for all. I do not say that with a Presto, Change!

the Social Revolution will make the Bowery tough a Chesterfield. But I do say that it will give to all mankind the material foundation upon which alone I aristocratic character can be built. I am a Socialist, not because I am an enemy of aristocracy, or because I undervalue it, but because I wish the proportion of aristocrats to reach the highest possible maximum.

Surely it is needless for me to point out to you that to-day commercialism has so tainted and polluted art, literature, and the drama, that most of our artists, fiction-writers, and play-wrights are mental prostitutes, and, saddest of all, some of them are so degraded that they do not even know they are prostitutes, but seriously talk of their art! I feel as though I were indulging in a platitude when I venture to remind you that it was because every Athenian freeman was a cultured and competent critic that sculpture and painting and the drama attained to such perfection in the days of Pericles. The socialistic ideal is that no man or woman, to say the least, shall be less cultivated than the average citizen of the Athens of Pericles. Today, as you know but too well, a play of the better sort can only be put on for an occasional matinee at an hour when our commercialized men cannot attend the theater, for to-day the only appreciable portion of the American community that has leisure to attain anything worthy of the name of culture is made up of the women of the upper classes.

If you wish to see better manners, more worthy fiction, higher art, and nobler drama, as I know you do, your only course is to become a Socialist comrade, and give us your aid in hastening the advent of the Social Revolution.

Will you do it?

Yours faithfully,
ROBERT RIVES LA MONTE.

MENCKEN'S REPLY TO LA MONTE'S FIRST LETTER

My Dear La Monte:

In one thing, at least, you and I are in agreement, and that is in our common belief that the world is by no means perfect. This, at first glance, seems to convict us of pessimism, but, as a matter of fact, we are thoroughgoing optimists, for both of us are firmly convinced that, however lamentable its present degree of imperfection, the world may, should, and will grow better. So far, indeed, we agree fully, but when we come to discuss the precise method and manner of this betterment, and to define the goal which lies ahead—when we strive, in brief, to lay bare the anatomy of human progress—our divergence, it quickly appears, is abysmal. Your ideal picture of the best possible world seems to me a very fair picture of the worst possible world, and I have no doubt that, until I convert you and lead you up to grace, *my* ideal picture, as I have sketched it elsewhere in the past, and as I shall try to draw it, bit by bit, once more, bears and will bear to you much the same aspect.

But before I go into an exposition of my own theory of progress, I want to point out to you a certain fault in the argument of your letter—a certain fault which seems to me to reach its maximum virulence to-day in the writings of Socialists, just as it reached a maximum sixty years ago in the writings of Christian theologians. It may be called, for want of a better label, a magnificent" faith in incredible evidence. At its worst, it leads to a ready acceptance of generalizations that are supported by nothing more logical than a wish that they were true. At its best, it seems to infect you Socialists with a willingness to adopt and defend any alleged fact or group of facts, however dubious, so long as it seems to prove your case.

This fault, my dear La Monte, is not peculiar to you, and I am firmly convinced that, if you are ever hanged, it will be for some other offense. As a matter of fact, I have found it in far more glorious flower in the compositions of those older and more enraptured Socialists whose works you have sent me, for the good of my soul, from time to time. But you are guilty, too, if only in the second or third degree, and this I hope to prove to you.

You begin the argument of your letter, for example, by quoting a government report, by which it appears that the average American workingman turns out $2,000 worth of goods a year, and gets $400 for his labor. I am utterly unable to verify these figures (in which embarrassment I am exactly on a footing with the statistician who fathers them), but they seem very plausible, and so I shall join you in accepting them. Your own belief in their accuracy is plainly without reservation, for you proceed to make them the foundation of your argument. "It is obvious," you say at the start, "that a man with $400 cannot purchase $2,000 worth of goods," and then you go on to examine this fact in the light of the Socialist philosophy, and to demonstrate its immorality. Setting aside, for the present, your final conclusions, I am perfectly willing to admit that you are right about the man with $400. His money will buy but $400 worth of goods, and this leaves $1,600 worth to be sold to someone else. Two interesting questions now arise. The one is, What other man buys this $1,600 worth? and the other is, What does this sum of $1,600 represent?

The second question is the more important, since a consideration of it reveals the answer to the first. Your answer to it, if I understand you rightly, is that the $1,600 represents the individual workingman's annual contribution to the nation's store of goods, over and above the amount he is able to buy back with his $400 and consume. This is what Karl Marx calls "surplus produce," and its value he calls "surplus value." You very properly observed that a surplus of $1,600 in every $2,000 is a very large one, and point out that, lacking a ready market, the accumulation of such surpluses is bound to get the nation into the unenviable position of a merchant with an enormous and unsaleable stock. In all of this your logic is sound enough, but you start out, unfortunately, from fallacious premises, for the surplus of $1,600 about which you and the government statisticians discourse in such alarm is almost entirely an academic myth. In a word, it has no actual existence, save in small part. Outside of books on political economy it is never heard of.

As a matter of sober fact—and I speak here from experience in one very typical line of manufacturing, as I shall show—the value of the average workman's contribution to the nation's store of goods, over and above the amount he buys back with his wages, is seldom equal to the value of the goods he thus buys back and consumes. The $400 man's contribution to the national surplus, far from being $1,600 a year, is probably little more than $160, and certainly a good deal less than $400. You assume that, by the mere exercise of his necromancy upon an empty void, he creates a value of $2,000, but here you assume altogether too much. What he really does do is this: he takes $1,200 worth, more or less, of raw material, adds to it (let us be generous and say) $800 worth of skill, and takes back $400 for his labor. His employer now owns a lot of goods which has cost him $1,600—$1,200 for raw material and $400 paid to the workman—and he offers it for sale at $2,000. The difference—$400—covers the Interest upon the employer's capital, the cost of selling the goods, the cost of light, heat, and taxes, and the cost of rent. Whatever is left over represents the employer's reasonable wage for his enterprise, industry, and skill. As I hope to show you later on, this wage is as much a true wage as the workman's, no matter how large it may be. But of this more anon.

What we have to consider here is the $1,200 worth of raw material. You may argue, I fear, that this is a preposterously excessive valuation, but let me assure you that it is not. It so happens that I once enjoyed, for three years, a rather intimate acquaintance with the workings of a successful cigar factory—a very typical example of the American manufacturing plant of moderate capital. Well, in that factory at the time, let us say, there was being produced a brand of cigars which cost about $22 a thousand to manufacture—I say "to manufacture" and not "to sell,"—and the workmen who made them were getting $6 a thousand for their labor. What did the balance of $16 represent? Was it the profit of the employer? Was it the workman's free contribution to the hoard of capital? Not at all! What it actually did represent was the cost of the material used by the workman in making cigars—of the raw material brought to the factory and made ready for the tables, with all duties, taxes, transportation, and insurance charges paid. It represented almost exactly the cost of producing the cigars, packed, stamped, and ready for the selling department—less the wages paid to the cigarmaker! This sum, you will note, was almost thrice the amount paid to the cigarmaker for the actual rolling of the cigars. Therefore, my assumption of a ratio of $400 to $1,200 in the preceding paragraphs was not without some justification in fact.

But what did the cost of the raw material, of the taxes, and of the packing represent? My answer is simple: it represented labor. The money paid for the actual tobacco represented the labor of the farmers who had wrung it from a reluctant earth, and the labor of the handlers and experts who had sorted it and cured it, and of the trainmen and mariners who had transported it. Without this labor, the tobacco would have had no existence; it was, literally, the incarnation of hours of toil. The money paid for it by the manufacturer went, in great part, straight back to these laborers. Putting the profits of landowners, of brokers, and of stockholders in transportation companies at the maximum, the laborers got at least a half. And the tale of the wood used in the boxes, of the labels pasted upon them, of the gum used to fasten the labels was the same. Again, it was the same with the money paid as taxes. It went directly into the hands of the government's employees, who were engaged, day and night, in producing that one commodity without which all other commodities cease to be—civilized security.

Therefore, let us assume that of all the $1,200 paid for raw material, $600 goes to workingmen as wages, and $600 goes to middlemen and capitalists as profits. We have yet to account for $800 of the $2,000, but of this, as we have seen, $400 goes to the workingman principally under consideration. There remains, then, after all else has been accounted for, the sum of $400. What is this? Are we to regard it as the profit of the manufacturer? In part, yes; but in part—no! It is profit, true enough, but it is gross profit, and out of it must come the cost of selling and of upkeep.

To get some notion of this cost, let us go back to our cigar factory. We saw there, you will recall, that a cigarmaker got $6 a thousand for making cigars, and that the raw material, brought to his table, together with the work of sorting and packing his cigars afterward, cost $16. This made the cost of the cigars, so far, $22 a thousand. The employer, let us say, got $30 a thousand for these cigars in his market, and his gross profit was thus $8 a thousand. But was his actual profit $8? By no means! It cost him, to begin, fully $3 a thousand to maintain his office and sell his goods, and he had to write off $1.50 more for bad bills, and another dollar or so for those expenses and hazards which no man can foresee. Who got the $3 charged to upkeep and selling costs? Practically every cent, I believe, went to workingmen—to coal miners for digging coal for his furnaces, to clerks for keeping his books, to salesmen for visiting his customers, to locomotive engineers for hauling his salesmen, to hotel cooks for cooking their meals, and so on ad infinitum. And the net profit that remained—what of that? I shall show you some day, I hope, that this was wages, too—the wages of the employer himself, paid to him for his skill at managing his capital, for his skill at buying raw material cheaply, and at inducing customers to buy his product, and for his skill, finally, at cajoling and coercing his workingmen into laboring for the $6 he paid them.

Now, to what have all of our figures brought us? Simply to this fact: that the $2,000 worth of goods produced by the $400 workman of your parable represents, not $400 worth of labor plus $1,600 worth of inflation, but $400 worth of labor plus at least $1,000 worth of other labor. The $400 man may be the principal actor in the drama, and his skill may be the principal factor in the conversion of sunlight and human energy into marketable commodities, but the men whose toil prepares his raw material and the men whose toil makes it possible for him to work at peace and sell his product have had their share, too. What remains over, after all of them have been paid, is very little. And so we come to a conclusion which makes all of your argument about panics, crises, and changing social orders vain, and it is this: that, while your $400 workman can buy back but $400 worth of the $2,000 worth of goods, *all* of the workmen who have had a hand in producing it are perfectly able to buy back, with their collective wages, nearly *all* of it. I am not much of a hand at statistics, but I venture the guess that in every $1,000 worth of goods produced under normal conditions in America to-day, fully $800 represents the wages of workmen. Thus your original surplus value of $1,600, which you regard with such trembling and in which you see such staggering portents, shrinks, on cold inspection, to $400!

No doubt you will say at once, as a good Marxian, that this surplus value, whether large or small, stands for capitalistic exploitation of the workingman, and that as such it is an evil. You may even argue, with Marx, that its evil lies, not in its actual size, but in its very existence—that any surplus value is immoral, and that the workingman should get all he produces. I shall try to answer this in a future letter, but meanwhile it may be well for me to record my earnest and enthusiastic dissent. As a matter of fact, the possibility of exploiting the workingman seems to me to be the one thing that justifies an optimistic view of human progress. It is this thing that gives existence a goal and a zest. It is this that insures to the human race all of those comforts and privileges which make it (at least in all save its lowest orders) superior to the race of milch cows. It is this that gives us the agreeable assurance that, however passionately we may occasionally embrace altruism, either as a religious creed or as a political doctrine, we are still being driven forward and upward, unceasingly and willy-nilly, by the irresistible operation of the law of natural selection.

Your facts and figures puzzle me in places other than the one we have been considering, not because they seem to me to prove anything, but because I find it utterly impossible to put any faith in their accuracy. You say in one paragraph, for instance: "Economics tell us that with all our male population between the ages of twentyfive and forty-five working three to four hours a day, we could produce enough to keep our whole population in such comfort as to-day requires an income of $5,000 a year." Let us look into this a bit, and see what it means. You have already laid it down, you will recall, that the average American workman earns $400 a year, and you say in your letter that "over fifty per cent. of our population actually belong to the working class." Let us suppose that the number is exactly fifty per cent., and that each man produces $2,000 worth of goods a year, as you say.

Well, then, you propose to restrict labor to those between twentyfive and forty-five, and so cut our working force in two by making idlers of those under twentyfive and those over forty-five. But at the same time you propose to double the force that re-mains by requiring every able-bodied person of the fifty per cent. now idle, between twentyfive and forty-five years old, to join the workers. Thus your working force will be substantially the same as it is at present.

But you then propose to reduce its working hours to "three or four" a day, and so divide its producing capacity by two. What will be the result? Simply that your workman's yearly output will be $1,000 worth of goods, instead of $2,000 worth, as at present, and that his income, even supposing him to get every cent of it back, will be but $1,000. On $1,000 a year how is he to obtain "such comfort as to-day requires an income of $5,000?"

In this I have given you the benefit of the doubt at every step. I have assumed, for instance, that fifty per cent. of the population is now made up of idlers, even though you yourself admit, in one place, that these idlers make up "but a handful of our people." I have assumed, too, that Socialism could achieve the impossible feat of paying for the same thing twice—of paying the farmer, that is, for raising tobacco, and then paying the cigarmaker for raising it. I have assumed everything you could desire, and yet I come to an absurdity at the end.

"Economics tell us," you say, and therein I see your fundamen-tal error. You have too much faith in the so-called science of eco-nomics, and you accept the wildest notions of its most extrava-gant sages as gospel truth. If "economics tell us" that our present army of workers, working half time, will be able, under Socialism, to earn twelve and a half times as much as at present—well, then, it is high time to demand proofs. My personal view is that no such proofs exist. The whole idea, in a word, is sheer nonsense. There is no more ground for it, in the actual facts of existence, than for the doctrine that, if I had brown eyes instead of blue, I would be a Methodist bishop at $8,000 a year.

The science of economics, as I understand it, is based upon a series of deductions from human experience. These deductions vary with the economist's education, environment, religion, and politics, and are often irreconcilable. In those departments of the science, indeed, in which the most distinguished professors have exercised their intellects, the divergence is most marked. I need only refer, in support of this, to the appalling debates regarding the currency which break forth every now and then. The conclusion a layman must necessarily derive from these debates is that the vast majority of experts are wrong. This conclusion grows firmer on reflection, for it is apparent that each economist's fiscal theory is but the deduction he has personally drawn from facts open to all. Therefore, why pay too much heed to him? Why not examine the facts themselves and evolve your own theories?

You may reply to this that my argument is foolish, and that its application to any other science—say pathology, for instance—will reveal its fatuity. My answer is that I am not applying it to pathology, for the facts of pathology are, in a sense, available only to the man specially trained to observe accurately. The facts of political economy, on the other hand, are the facts of everyday life. If my meaning is not clear, let me direct your attention to Adam Smith's Theory of Rents and Ehrlich's Theory of Immunity. If you will find me one man, of average intelligence and education, who fails to understand Smith at his first reading, I will give you a dollar. If, on the other hand, you find me one man, of average intelligence and education, who understands Ehrlich on a first reading, I will give you another dollar. The one requires only a reasonable degree of sanity; the other requires special training and a wealth of actual experience.

For these reasons I am chary of accepting economic theories, and much prefer the evidence to the verdict. I have no doubt that the gentleman who prepared the government report you quote was an expert hired at enormous expense, and yet I can't rid myself of the notion that the money paid to him was wasted.

But I must have done with this series of objections to your authorities, else this letter will have exhausted you without any statement of the creed I propose to offer in opposition to Socialism. This creed consists, first and last, in a firm belief in the beneficence and permanence of the evolutionary process. I believe, in other words, that the human race is incomparably the highest race of beings at present existing in the world, and I believe further that, as the years come and go, its superiority to the lower races of animals is growing constantly greater. I believe that you and I are far superior men, in many ways, to our great-grandfathers, and that our superiority over Christopher Columbus, Julius Cæsar, and Moses, in many more ways, is infinite.

But what do I mean by superiority? What, in other words, is my definition of progress? Naturally enough, it is hard to frame such a definition in a few words, but I may throw some light upon my notion of the thing itself by showing how it is to be measured. Progress, then, as I see it, is to be measured by the accuracy of man's knowledge" of nature's forces. If you examine this sentence carefully you will observe that I conceive progress as a sort of process of disillusion. Man gets ahead, in other words, by discarding the theory of to-day for the fact of to-morrow. Moses believed that the earth was flat, Cæsar believed that his family doctor could cure pneumonia, and Columbus believed that devils often entered into harmless old women and turned them into witches, and that the lightning was a bomb hurled by a wrathful God at sinful man. You and I, knowing that all three of these distinguished men were wrong in their beliefs, are their superiors to that extent.

Now, all the illusions which have afflicted the human race since its days of nonage may be divided into two classes. First come those which have arisen out of the imperfection of our powers of perception; and secondly come those that have arisen out of errors made in the interpretation of facts accurately observed. An excellent example of the first class is the familiar doctrine, held today by the ignorant, and until very recently by all, that the disease called malaria is caused by breathing impure air. Tested by the evidence of the naked eye, this doctrine seemed entirely sound. But by and by men began to use microscopes to aid their eyes, and one day, seized by a happy thought, an enterprising man took the trouble to place a drop of blood from a malaria patient's veins beneath his glass. Since then the old doctrine has been put aside forever by all whose beliefs are worth hearing, and we know that malaria is caused, not by impure air, but by various minute parasites of the class of *sporozoa*. The human race, within historic times, has rejected thousands of delusions of this class, but many yet remain. As we perfect apparatus to reinforce our dull senses they will go overboard, one by one.

The delusions and illusions of the second class resolve themselves into two grand, or king delusions. One of them is the notion that a human being, by his words or acts, is capable of suspending or modifying the immutable laws which govern" the universe. The other is the notion that a human being is able to make laws for himself which shall have the force of the immutable laws aforesaid. Out of the first of these delusions springs the doctrine of the efficacy of prayer, and with it all of the world's vast and bizarre stock of religions. Out of the second springs the ancient science of morality, with all its multitude of efforts to combat the eternal and inexorable law that the strong shall prevail over the weak. The latest of such efforts is comprehended in the political theory called Socialism. It is the most fatuous of the whole lot, for it proposes, not only to make human laws as immutable as natural laws, but actually to make them supersede and nullify those natural laws. Here, indeed, we behold human beings on the topmost pinnacle of bombastic folly. I can imagine no more stupendous egotism.

In this you may perceive, though perhaps only dimly, for my exposition may be none too clear, the reasons which impel me to decline your invitation to join your crusade. I am no apologist | for the existing order of things. Like Huxley, I believe that the management of the universe is by no means perfect, but such as it is, we must accept it. If you point out that human progress, as I have defined it, involves the practical enslavement of two-thirds of the human race, my answer is that I can't help it. If you point out that a slave always runs the risk of being oppressed by a particularly cruel master, I answer that a master always runs the risk of having his brains knocked out by a particularly enterprising slave. If you point out that, by my scheme of progress, it is only the upper stratum that actually progresses, I answer that only the upper stratum is capable of progressing unaided.

The mob is inert and moves ahead only when it is dragged or driven. It clings to its delusions with a pertinacity that is appalling. A geological epoch is required to rid it of a single error, and it is so helpless and cowardly that every fresh boon it receives, every lift upon its slow journey upward, must come to it as a free gift from its betters—as a gift not only free, but also forced. Great men have fought and died for the truth for a thousand years, and yet the average low-caste white man of to-day, throughout Christendom, still believes that Friday is an unlucky day, still believes that ghosts walk the earth, and still holds to an immovable faith in signs, portents, resurrections, redemptions, miracles, prophecies, hells, gehennas, and political panaceas.

It may be true that the existing order of things demands bloody human sacrifices, but, so far as I am able to see it, the thing is inevitable. Whatever you may say against it, you cannot deny that the existing order of things at least produces progress. It produced, for instance, a Pasteur, and if, directly and indirectly, in the course of long ages, a million serfs had to be used up to make this Pasteur possible, I, for one, believe that the result was worth the cost. The work that Pasteur did in the world put the clock of time ahead a hundred years, and conferred a permanent and constantly cumulative benefit upon the whole human race, freeman and slave alike, now and forevermore. Would the lives of a million serfs have been of equal value? Not at all! They would have given to the world only the matter and energy that they took out of it, and their influence on progress, if they exerted any influence at all, would have been reactionary.

You latter-day Socialists have all sorts of excuses and compromises to offer. You say, for instance, that under Socialism the Pasteurs of the world would be cherished and encouraged just as much as under the law of natural selection. But the objection to this is that, after two generations of Socialism, there would be no more Pasteurs. To produce the things the world needs to-day and to-morrow we must have workmen who toil. But to produce the things that will make the world a hundred years hence a better place to live in than the world of to-day we must have men who, by exploiting, either directly or indirectly, the work of these toilers, may have the ease and leisure to make great plannings and to find out great truths.

Yours sincerely,
H. L. MENCKEN.

LA MONTE'S SECOND LETTER

My Dear Mencken:

I have derived infinite delight from your sanguine letter. Although your statistics have confused me where they have not amused me, the latter part of your letter has made my future task far easier by helping me to place your mental position chronologically. I have no intention of being offensive when I tell you that you appear to me to belong in part to the Greece of Pericles and in part to the France of Diderot.

When you assert that it is necessary to exploit and dehumanize millions of proletarians in order to produce here and there a Pasteur or two, you merely paraphrase the defense of human slavery that we find again and again, now explicit and now implicit, in the works of Aristotle, Plato, and Xenophon. In their mouths the argument was a good one, for in their times the productivity of human labor was so pitifully small that only by keeping hordes in slavery was it possible for any to enjoy the leisure requisite for the attainment of culture. But, though you, my dear Mencken, live in an age when steam and electricity have been harnessed by man, you still repeat arguments that were obsolescent in the days of Cicero; for Antiparos, a Greek poet of that era, saw in the invention of the water-mill the promise that humanity might be freed from the curse of slavery, and sang thus in praise of the leisure that gracious Demeter was bestowing upon mankind:—

"Spare the arm which turns the mill, O millers, and sleep peacefully. Let the cock warn you in vain that the day is breaking. Demeter has imposed upon the nymphs the labor of the slaves, and behold them leaping merrily over the wheel, and behold the axle-tree, shaken, turning with its spokes and making the heavy-rolling stone revolve. Let us live the life of our fathers, and let us rejoice in idleness over the gifts that the Goddess grants us."

How many eons does it take for a Mencken to catch up to an Antiparos?

When you measure progress by the increase of accurate knowledge, and thus apotheosize human reason, you reproduce perfectly the spirit that animated Rousseau and Diderot and the great French Encyclopedists. In the words of Engels, "the French philosophers of the eighteenth century, the forerunners of the Revolution, appealed to reason as the sole judge of all that is. A rational government, rational society, were to be founded; everything that ran counter to eternal reason was to be remorselessly done away with." When once this was done, all would be for the best in the best of all possible worlds. This was an entirely justifiable conception in their day. But since then the experiment has been tried; the French Revolution has turned Christendom upside down, and the Third Estate has been enthroned in every civilized land; but the reality attained is far from corresponding to the noble dreams of the great French materialists of the eighteenth century. Most of us have learned something from this experience, and have begun to suspect that human progress is more dependent upon the development of the processes whereby human stomachs are filled and human backs are covered than it is upon the increase of academic knowledge. But you, dear child of the eighteenth century, continue to compose in unruffled serenity your charming odes to Eternal Reason.

Possibly you will understand now why I smile when I read your profession of faith, "that you and I are far superior men, in many ways, to our great-grandfathers, and that our superiority over Christopher Columbus, Julius Cæsar, and Moses, in many more ways, is infinite."

Do you think I am unreasonable in asking this superior twentieth century man to produce some arguments against Socialism, not borrowed bodily from the Greece of Pericles and the France of Rousseau?

In my first letter I introduced a few figures merely to illustrate and make plain my argument. Your letter leads me to believe that instead of serving the purpose I had intended, they have on the contrary confused you and obscured my argument. This is not to be wondered at, as I am no statistician and have always found figures a burden. In order to make my position quite clear, I hope you will permit me to recapitulate my argument without figures.

The object of introducing improved methods of production, such as machinery, is, as Antiparos clearly saw two thousand years ago, to save labor. If the work done by any given machine does not cost its owner less than it would cost him to have the same labor done by men and women by the former methods, the machine will not be used. But, in a society where the different producers of goods sell competitively on the market, each individual owner of a productive plant is driven, whether he likes or not, to make continuous improvements in his machinery. If he does not he will be undersold and driven into bankruptcy. Every such improvement means an increase in the product relatively to the wages paid out in that establishment, so that the proportion of the total product in society at large, that is in excess of the quantity that the wage-earners are able to purchase for their own consumption, is growing and must continue to grow until it eventually reaches such proportions as to compel a Social Revolution. The more developed is the mechanical equipment, the industrial technique of a country, the larger becomes the proportion of the national produce that the working-class are unable to purchase; in other words, the smaller becomes the fraction of their own product that the workers receive. For this reason the workers of England and Germany receive a far smaller fraction of the product of their labor than do the workers of the comparatively backward countries, such as Italy, Spain, and Portugal; and the American workers of 1908 are able to buy a much smaller fraction of the product of their labor than could the American workers of 1850. You will kindly note that I did not advance in my former letter, and I do not advance now, any argument based on the immorality of such an arrangement. I would think as readily of questioning the morality of the law of gravitation. It matters very little to my argument just what the exact share of the workers may be at any given time, but what my argument is based on is the constant decrease in the ratio between the purchasing power of the working-class and the value of the total national product; and this ratio must decrease as long as we continue to improve our machinery, and competition makes such improvement of our industrial technique imperative. As I said in my first letter, it is the "progressive and inexorable change in the technical composition of capital that makes a Social Revolution inevitable."

The figures as to average wages and product per worker that I used for illustrative purposes in my former letter were quoted by memory from Tables 1 and 2 in Census Bulletin No. 150.[1] This Bulletin No. 150 is based on manufactures alone, and shows the average wages to be $432, and the product per worker to be something in excess of $2,000. The figures in these census bulletins are gathered chiefly to show the growth of industry, and for other commercial purposes, and not to meet the needs of economic study, so that it is somewhat difficult, if not impossible, to ascertain just what elements other than the new value added by the worker this $2,000 contains. Lucien Sanial, of Northport, Long Island, one of our ablest statisticians, has made a careful study of the census of 1900 in connection with Bradstreet's and Dun's reports, and other sources, and his conclusion is that our

---

1   Second edition, September 15, 1902.

total product in 1900 was $24,500,000,000, and the total value of the laborpower used in its production, $5,815,000,000, and that the portion of the product that Labor was in a position to purchase was 23.74 per centum.

It should be remembered that the workers purchase everything at the very highest retail prices, while the value of product given in the census is based on factory prices; so that in order to ascertain how much of the product the workers can purchase, one must add to the census valuation of the product a certain percentage to cover the cost of transporting the product to market and the costs of distribution in the form of wholesale and retail profits. I have found by calculation that the percentage thus added by Mr. Sanial was forty-two per cent. Using this percentage, I have figured from Census Bulletin No. 150 the workers' share of the total value of our manufactured product at every decade from 1850 to 1900. Even if this percentage is not accurate, it does not vitiate my conclusion that the share of the workers is decreasing, for the calculation for each tenth year is made on exactly the same basis. Here are my results tabulated:—

Percentage of product workers could purchase in...					1850...	36.1
"	"	"	"	"	1860...	31.2
"	"	"	"	"	1870...	31.3
"	"	"	"	"	1880...	33.7
"	"	"	"	"	1890...	30.5
"	"	"	"	"	1900...	27.0

You will of course at once note that the workers' share rose 2.4 per centum in the decade from 1870 to 1880, but if we turn to the figures for capital invested in manufacture, we will find that in that decade the capital invested only rose from $2,118,208,769 to $2,790,272,606, which was scarcely enough to keep abreast of the growth of population, so that as a matter of fact there was little, if any, advance in industrial technique during that decade, while in the decade from 1850 to 1860, when Labor's share decreased nearly five per centum, the capital invested nearly doubled, growing from $533,245,351 to $1,009,855,715, showing a tremendous improvement in machinery.

I have no idea that these figures are strictly correct, but I think that they do show beyond cavil that the purchasing power of the working-class is, to say the least, growing constantly more inadequate to perform its economic function in a society based on private ownership of the means of production. If we take the figures for particular industries, the same result is more strikingly brought out. Fred D. Warren of Girard, Kansas, has extracted from the "Eighteenth Annual Report of the Commissioner of Labor" the following information in regard to the pig-iron industry:

	1870	1880	1890	1900
Product per man (in tons)...	66	81	260	395
Average wages...	$453	$304	$460	$506
Average profit made from each worker...	$322	$360	$405	$900

I take it that pig-iron is a far more typical modern industry than is the cigar-making industry, which you discuss, as the latter has been far less revolutionized by machinery and chemistry. At any rate, I do not feel competent to enter upon a discussion of the cigar business, as my only connection with it has been that of a consumer—when Fortune smiled—and you give no source of your statistics save your own experience; so that I am compelled to leave this field to you.

You will, I think, admit that by the methods of economists and statisticians I have shown that there is a growing surplus of goods, and that the disposition of this surplus constitutes a very real difficulty, even if you are not ready to admit that it is of itself sufficient to compel a Social Revolution. But, curiously enough, you, the panegyrist of Eternal Reason, who measure progress by the growth of accurate knowledge, distrust this same human intelligence when it is applied to economics and sociology, and would appear to hold that in this one domain more credence is to be given to the man in the street than to the man with trained intelligence who has devoted years to the study of these very questions. I am free to admit that it is rather disconcerting for an opponent of Socialism who looks for the increase of knowledge to bring about a Nietzschean millennium to find that knowledge of economics is in inverse ratio to prejudice against Socialism—that as the former rises, the latter melts away. But this seems to be the sad fact. Listen to this tale of woe poured out not long ago by Leslie M. Shaw, ex-Secretary of the Treasury, at an alumni dinner of Dickinson College at the Hotel Saint Denis in New York.

"Socialism is being taught on every hand, and I am alarmed by the general trend of things in this connection. At our Chautauquas the lecturers are all preaching the doctrine. Teachers of Sociology in our schools and colleges are doing the same thing. With a few exceptions, they are Socialists, as you can find out by a few moments of conversation with them; and the exceptions are anarchists.

"Our public libraries are full of socialistic literature. Why, in a large city recently, where there was a strike, the reading-room was packed day after day with all kinds of people. When the librarian was asked what they were reading, he replied: 'Socialism, every one of them. There is not a book on Socialism in any language that is not here.'

"Sociology, as it is taught in our colleges, is nothing more than a fad—and a dangerous one, too. You cannot build up men's minds with fads. Mr. Wilshire, the socialistic editor, recently asked a friend of mine if he would arrange for a joint debate on

Socialism with a professor in one of our large universities. When my friend went to the professor, the latter said:

"'No, I won't debate on Socialism, because Wilshire and I agree.'

"Even the pulpit nowadays reflects some socialistic doctrines, and it is too bad."

No doubt Mr. Shaw would agree with you that the troublesome "surplus" of goods about which I "and the government statisticians discourse in such alarm is almost entirely an academic myth"; that, in a word, "it has no actual existence, save in small part," that "outside of books on political economy it is never heard of." But both you and he would have to admit that Chauncey M. Depew's reputation for virginal ignorance of economics is spotless, and yet Senator Depew in what many of his fellow-citizens call "his great speech" at the Republican Convention of 1900 in Philadelphia, that renominated President McKinley, said: "We produce in this great country of ours every year $2,500,000,000 more of goods than we can consume." It seems that knowledge of the existence of that surplus had leaked outside of purely academic circles eight years ago. And the New York *Sun* of December 20, 1908, contained a long letter from Berlin, explaining that the reason there had been at that time so much adverse criticism of the Kaiser was that Germany had been passing through a severe business crisis, and that therefore many indiscreet acts of his majesty that would have been passed over lightly in prosperous times had been the target for the most venomous attacks. Here is one sentence from this letter which I commend to your careful attention: "Existing markets are crowded with wares for which there are no profitable buyers."

In Germany it would appear that even newspapermen had heard of this troublesome surplus, which, in the opinion of the writer of the *Sun* letter, must sooner or later drive Germany into a war with England in her desperate struggle to find an outlet into which she can pour this plethora of commodities.

Robert Rives La Monte & H. L. Mencken

I think it is now evident that knowledge of this pestilential superabundance is not confined to economists, statisticians, and Socialists. I think that the figures I have already given you prove it to be a most pregnant reality. It may be well for me to say that in preparing my figures of the workers' share of the product of our manufacturing industries for 1850, 1860, 1870, 1880, 1890, and 1900, I, in every instance, deducted from the total value of the product as given in the Census, first, the value of the partially manufactured goods used as materials in those industries, and, second, the value of the true raw materials used in them, so that my figures represented as nearly as possible nothing but the new value added by the workers in the process of manufacture. But, if you will still remain skeptical about the real existence of this "academic myth," permit me to quote to you a few figures from the "Fifth Annual Report of the United States Steel Corporation for the Fiscal Year ended December 31, 1906," which, thanks to the kindness of Fred D. Warren, is lying before me as I write.

From page 5, I quote:

> "The total net earnings of all properties after deducting expenditures for ordinary repairs and maintenance (approximately $28,000,000), employees' bonus funds, and also interest on bonds and fixed charges of the subsidiary companies, amounted to—$156,624,273.18."

On page 24 the average number of employees for the same year (1906) on all the properties of the Corporation is given as 202,457, and the total annual *salaries* and wages as $147,765,540.

If you add together the net profits (from which you will note all possible deductions have been made), and the wages (which include the princely salaries of the Steel Trust officials), you will find that the profits are 51.46 per cent. of the whole and the wages are 48.54 per cent.

Of course the Steel Trust profits are figured on the basis of factory prices for the product, which accounts for this apparently high ratio of the workers' share to the total. Allowing for this fact, these figures agree fairly closely with those for our manufactures in general which I have made above from Bulletin 150.

But I care not what the exact percentage may be. The fact that this Steel Trust report establishes beyond a peradventure is that there is a tremendous surplus to be marketed.

In discussing the cigar business, after allowing for "interest upon the employer's capital, the cost of selling the goods, the cost of light, heat, taxes, and the cost of rent" and various other items you say: "Whatever is left over represents the employer's reasonable wage for his enterprise, industry, and skill. As I hope to show you later on, this wage is as much a true wage as the workman's, no matter how large it may be."

Let me call your attention to the fact that every particle of "enterprise, industry, and skill" used in managing and superintending the vast business of the Steel Trust is furnished by salaried employees, and that those salaries for "enterprise, industry, and skill" are included in the wage account I have quoted, and that after this "true wage," as you call it, has been paid in full and most liberally, our old friend "the Troublesome Surplus" still stands there, with undiminished girth, smiling at us, and asking, "Well, and what are you going to do with me?" Do you not think he is entitled to a serious answer?

The answer our captains of industry have been making for the past few years, as I pointed out in my former letter, has been to devote capital more and more to the improvement and enlargement of what we may call our permanent industrial and transportation plant, but while this effectively relieves the symptoms of distress for the time being, it unfortunately aggravates the disease in the long run by facilitating production and transportation. There are two other answers you may be tempted to make: one is that it is possible for the leisure class to increase its wasteful expenditure sufficiently to meet the requirements of the case, the other is that war and calamity may intervene and cause an adequate destruction of goods. Professor Thorstein Veblen has discussed both of these possible remedies very interestingly in his remarkable book, "The Theory of Business Enterprise". His conclusions are that it is out of the question for private extravagance and waste to be raised to an adequate pitch, but that we may look hopefully to war and calamity as palliatives.

"The persistent defection of reasonable profits," he says, in discussing the former point, "calls for a remedy. The remedy may be sought in one or the other of two directions: (1) in an increased unproductive consumption of goods; or (2) in an elimination of that 'cutthroat' competition that keeps profits below the 'reasonable' level. If enough of the work or of the output is turned to wasteful expenditures, so as to admit of but a relatively slight aggregate saving, as counted by weight and tale, profitable prices can be maintained on the old basis of capitalization. If the waste is sufficiently large, the current investment in industrial equipment will not be sufficient to lower prices appreciably through competition.

"Wasteful expenditure on a scale adequate to offset the surplus productivity of modern industry is nearly out of the question. Private initiative cannot carry the waste of goods and services to nearly the point required by the business situation. Private waste is no doubt large, but business principles, leading to saving and shrewd investment, are too ingrained in the habits of modern men to admit an effective retardation of the rate of saving. Something more to the point can be done, and indeed is being done, by the civilized governments in the way of effectual waste. Armaments, public edifices, courtly and diplomatic establishments, and the like, are almost altogether wasteful, so far as bears on the present question.

"The waste of time and effort that goes into military service, as well as the employment of the courtly, diplomatic, and ecclesiastical personnel, counts effectually in the same direction. But however extraordinary this public waste of substance latterly has been, it is apparently altogether inadequate to offset the surplus productivity of the machine industry, particularly when this productivity is seconded by the great facility which the modern business organization affords for the accumulation of savings in relatively few hands. There is also the drawback that the waste of time involved in military service reduces the purchasing power of the classes that are drawn into the service, and so reduces the amount of wasteful consumption which these classes might otherwise accomplish.

"So long as industry remains at its present level of efficiency, and especially so long as incomes continue to be distributed somewhat after the present scheme, waste cannot be expected to overtake production, and can therefore not check the untoward tendency to depression."[2]

But what waste is unable to do for us, war fortunately has proved itself able to accomplish. But is the present generation of men, who, you tell us, are infinitely superior to Christopher Columbus, Julius Cæsar, and Moses, going to remain long contented with a system that depends for its perpetuation on the frequent recurrence of war, fire, earthquake, and calamity?

What war has done for us of late is well brought out by Veblen in the following passage:—

"Since the seventies as an approximate date and as applying particularly to America and in a less degree to Great Britain, the course of affairs in business has apparently taken a permanent change as regards crises and depression. During this recent period, and with increasing persistency, chronic depression has been the rule rather than the exception in business. Seasons of easy times, 'ordinary prosperity,' during this period are pretty uniformly traceable to specific causes extraneous to the process of industrial business proper. In one case, the early nineties, it seems to have been a pe-

---

2 "The Theory of Business Enterprise", Thorstein Veblen (Scribners', New York, 1904) pp. 255-258.

culiar crop situation, and in the most notable case of a speculative inflation, the one now (1904) apparently drawing to a close, it was the Spanish-American War, coupled with the expenditures for stores, munitions, and services incident to placing the country on a war footing, that lifted the depression and brought prosperity to the business community. If the outside stimulus from which the present prosperity takes its impulse be continued at an adequate pitch, the season of prosperity may be prolonged; otherwise there seems little reason to expect any other outcome than a more or less abrupt and searching liquidation."[3]

This was written in 1904. We were soon blessed with the Russo-Japanese War, the San Francisco Earthquake, and the Baltimore Fire, so that the "stimulus" was "continued at an adequate pitch," and the " season of prosperity" was "prolonged" until November, 1907, when there occurred "a more or less abrupt and searching liquidation." In spite of his unfortunate handicap of an unusually thorough knowledge of political economy, do you not think Professor Veblen was able to make a fairly accurate analysis of the situation?

Relying upon my own far more limited knowledge of economics, I have no hesitation in predicting that the present period of depression will last at least seven years unless (1) in the meantime the "increase of accurate knowledge" or the hard facts of adversity lead us to establish the Cooperative Commonwealth, or (2) unless a great war, such as the *Sun* (N. Y.) Berlin correspondent suggests between Germany and England, breaks out. I confess the second alternative appears to me to be far the more probable.

This letter is already so unconscionably long that I can but touch upon the question of the probable hours of labor and the standard of comfort in the society of the future. In my former

---

3   "The Theory of Business Enterprise", Thorstein Veblen (Scribners', New York, 1904) pp. 250-251.

letter I suggested that from three to four hours a day with all the male population between the ages of twenty-five and forty-five working usefully would suffice to keep all our people in such comfort as to-day requires an income of $5,000 a year. This arouses your incredulity, naturally enough, and you devote several pages to proving its impossibility. Perhaps I should have made it plainer that I had in mind the income per family, and not per capita. But, had I done so, I doubt not my statement would have appeared scarcely less incredible to you. One fundamental difficulty is that the life of the future—such a life as is pictured in William Morris' "News from Nowhere"—is in all respects so different from life

> "In the days of the years we dwell in,
> that wear our lives away,"

that the two quantities are really incommensurable, but I can think of no feasible way of giving you an idea of the standard of comfort that I believe will be universal in "the wonderful days a-coming when all shall be better than well" save by suggesting in dollars an income that enables an American family to-day to approach a similar standard of comfort and well-being—I say "approach," because I do not believe any income, however large, will to-day make possible the joy of living that will be world-wide in the wonderful days to be. My own opinion is that in my former letter I named too low a figure. In many of our cities today it takes $5,000 a year to pay the rent of such a house as every family ought to demand.

The trouble with your mathematical demonstration of my folly is that you make no allowance for the amount of labor that is now wasted by the anarchy of our competitive system. The simplest illustration of this is the oft-used milk-business. Count the number of wagons delivering milk on your block some morning, and compare it with the number of postmen delivering letters, and you will begin to form some faint idea of the vast aggregate of unnecessary labor that is being done to-day. I believe it impossible to estimate exactly the quantity of this wasted labor that could be eliminated under a co-operative system. Sidney A. Reeve, in his book "The Cost of Competition"[4], states that the amount of labor thus wasted is at least double that actually usefully employed in production. I do not vouch for the accuracy of this calculation, but I am sure you will feel the more inclined to give it credence when I gladly assure you that Mr. Reeve is not an economist. I have ascertained by reference to "Who's Who" that he was Professor of Steam and Hydraulic Engineering at Worcester Polytechnic Institute from 1896 to 1906, and Lecturer on Steam Engineering at Harvard University in 1907. These subjects would seem to me to require an aptitude for acquiring your *summum bonum*, accurate knowledge.

Another vast economy we will make, and that you did not take into consideration, is to close up all the smaller and more poorly equipped plants, and do all our work in the most perfect plants that science can devise. The trusts have already begun this process for us. The Sugar Trust closed up about seventy-five per cent. of the plants it controlled a few years ago, and the Whiskey Trust put out of operation sixty-eight distilleries out of eighty. It is impossible to set a limit to the economy possible in this direction.

I believe it impossible to prove my estimate accurate, but I feel sure that a very little thought along the lines I have suggested will convince you that it is distinctly *moderate*.

Professor Hertzka of Austria some years ago in his "Laws of Social Evolution" calculated what the (then) 22,000,000 people of Austria might do, if properly organized.

"It takes," he estimates, "26,250,000 acres of agricultural land, and 7,500,000 of pasturage, for all agricultural products.

---

4   "The Cost of Competition", Sidney A. Reeve (McClure, Phillips & Co., New York, 1906).

Then I allowed a house to be built for every family, consisting of five rooms. I found that all industries, agriculture, architecture, building, flour, sugar, coal, iron, machine-building, and chemical production, need 615,000 laborers employed eleven hours per day, 300 days a year, to satisfy every imaginable want for 22,000,000 inhabitants.

"These 615,000 laborers are only 12.3 per cent. of the population able to do work, excluding women and all persons under sixteen or over fifty years of age; all these latter to be considered as not able.

"Should all the 5,000,000 able-bodied men in the country be engaged in work, instead of 615,000, they need only to work 36.9 days every year to produce everything needed for the support of the population of Austria. But should the 5,000,000 work all the year, say 300 days—which they would probably have to do to keep the supply fresh in every department—each one would only work one hour and twenty-two and a half minutes per day.

"But to engage to produce all the *luxuries*, in addition, would take, in round figures, 1,000,000 workers, classed and assorted as above, or only twenty per cent. of all those able, excluding every woman, or every person under sixteen or over fifty, as before. The 5,000,000 able, strong male members could produce everything imaginable for the whole nation of 22,000,000 in two hours and twelve minutes per day, working 300 days a year."

It is nearly impossible to judge of the accuracy of such an estimate, but there are some accurate data forthcoming to show what we could do in this country. J. L. Franz has shown by figures taken from the "Thirteenth Annual Report of the Commissioner of Labor"[5] for 1898 that by using the methods actually used on the big western wheat farms in 1898, to produce the wheat (350,000,000 bushels) actually used for home consumption in

---

5   Washington, 1899

1898, would have required only the labor of 1,000,000 persons working one hour a day on every week-day of the year.[6]

Work to-day is such a curse that it is very natural and pardonable to hail extremely short hours of labor as the chiefest of blessings, but we err in doing so, for, as my good friend, Henry L. Slobodin of New York, reminded me in a letter the other day, "those who emphasize the short hours of labor which will be necessary in future society as a great advantage miss the point of the Socialist position. The modern Socialist's position is that whereas labor is and is considered at present a hardship and almost a calamity, in the future it will be a glad and joyous exercise of natural functions. The tendencies which may be perceived now in a very weak form are to make labor pleasant and attractive. On the other hand, there is a tendency to make pleasures useful. These two tendencies converge and will meet in the society of the future. So that generally speaking in the future all labor will be more of a pleasure than the pleasures are now, and the pleasures of the future will be more productive than the labor is now. From that point of view, to discuss how short the hours of labor will be in the future is unnecessary."

Space will not permit me to take up here your startling assertion that "after two generations of Socialism, there would be no more Pasteurs." Surely you do not mean to contend that adversity and penury are favorable to the development of scientific genius, and that by abolishing poverty we will make the genesis of genius impossible? But I am comforted by the thought that, even if you are right, and we are to produce no more Pasteurs in the society of the future, at any rate we shall have far less need for them than we have to-day. When we shall have definitely abolished poverty from the earth those medical and chemical savants who have hitherto found their chief occupation in devising means of fighting or curing diseases that are in large part the products, direct

---

6   See *International Socialist Review*, Vol. I, p. 357.

or indirect, of poverty and the filth caused by poverty, will have leisure to devote to devising chemical processes for performing the dirty work which is to-day done by cheap and dirty men and women. They will also find a fertile field in discovering chemical methods of producing nutritive substances.

How the abolition of poverty will compel our Pasteurs to change their occupations was strikingly brought home to his hearers by Dr. Linsly Williams of the Vanderbilt Clinic in a speech he made before the delegates of the Brooklyn Central Labor Union in the Auditorium Hall of the Museum of Natural History. The occasion was Brooklyn Labor Union Day of the International Tuberculosis Exhibition. I quote briefly from the newspaper account of his speech:

"Dr. Williams began by saying that although everybody was more or less affected by the ravages of tuberculosis, the working class suffered particularly, as thirty-three per cent. of the workers died from the dread disease. . . . Then, striking the keynote of his discourse, the doctor declared that the greatest predisposing cause of the white plague was low wages and working under unsanitary conditions. He told of the unhealthful way in which a great deal of the work of the world was done, and as a proof of his statements said that while the average annual death rate per thousand from tuberculosis was two and a half for the general public, the rate for stone-cutters was 5.4, for cigar-makers 5.3, and for printers, 4.3, with the majority of the workers in the other trades also above the average rate. On the other hand, the death rate for doctors was 1.6, and for farmers only 1.1.

"In conclusion Dr. Williams made an impressive plea for cleanliness and concerted effort in the work of fighting the white plague, and also took occasion to score those 'superior' individuals who calmly assert that everybody can be clean and have fresh air if they want to. 'It is easy to tell people to be clean,' said he, 'but when one has to work long hours for low wages I tell you it is almost impossible to be clean and have plenty of fresh air. When people are huddled together in the crowded tenements it is no easy thing to take a bath, and if one opens the windows for air, instead of real air, a volume of smoke and dirt makes one close them again. The main thing in this fight is to get better pay for your labor so that you can live in better houses and have better food and thus be enabled to resist the attacks of the disease.'"

There are several other things I would like to say to you in regard to this Pasteur argument of yours, but they will have to wait for another letter, as this one is already far too long. I hope you will pardon its excessive length and believe me when I promise not to sin in this particular way again.

Let me hear from you soon.

Faithfully,
R. R. LA MONTE.

MENCKEN'S REPLY TO LA MONTE'S SECOND LETTER

My Dear La Monte:

When I dropped my last epistle into the letter box there went with it a pious hope that the modest *reductio ad absurdum* I had attempted might rescue you from your maze of fantastic statistics, or, at least, that it might implant in you a certain salutary distrust of statisticians. But I see now that this hope was a vain thing, and doomed to an early death, for you return to the attack, with figures that are even more fantastic than those you discharged in your first salvo. Perhaps, however, I have no right to dispute these figures in such an offhand manner, for I have no doubt that, at bottom, there may be a good deal of truth in them. But I am on the safe side, I believe, when I maintain that, whatever their degree of accuracy may be, you and your Socialist friends demand no proof of it, but take it on trust, and that the deductions you draw from them show a great deal more enthusiasm than logic.

You begin, for instance, by summoning to the witness stand a professor from faraway Austria, and he, in turn, starts out by announcing a discovery. He has found, he says, that a lot of energy is wasted in Austria, and that the work of that country, which now engages all but a small minority of its inhabitants, might be done very well by comparatively few of them. Following the custom of statisticians, he does not offer us the facts upon which this conclusion is based, but as for the conclusion itself, he is very sure of its truth. Given an eleven-hour workday, he says, and 300 workdays a year, and it would be possible for 615,000 Austrians to provide all the necessities of life for the 22,000,000 inhabitants of the empire. From this he reaches the conclusion that, if 5,000,000 men lent a hand (there are just about 5,000,000 able-bodied men of working age in the empire), instead of but 615,000, each man would have to labor but one hour and twenty-two and a half minutes a day.

All of this makes an interesting experiment in simple arithmetic, but when you cite it, in all seriousness, as proof of your argument that, under Socialism, the average workingman of America, working but three or four hours a day, would earn $5,000 a year, you exhibit a lamentable inability to differentiate between the possible and the probable, the abstract and the actual, the conceivable and the ponderable. Your Austrian professor discourses so glibly, not of real human beings, but of algebraic x's of his own creation, and you follow him in mistaking these x's for men and women. He sets aside, as of no account whatever, almost every one of the multitude of yearnings, ambitions, desires, and appetites which distinguish man from the red ant, and you follow him in holding them to be negligible. He draws figures on a slate—and you assume they are alive.

It would take a long letter to show, in detail, how widely your professor's elaborate syllogism varies from the facts of existence. I need only point out here the absurdity of supposing that it would be possible to find 5,000,000 men who would be at once capable of doing their work efficiently, and willing to do it, day after day, even for but an hour and a half a day, without some effort to rid themselves of the necessity for doing it at all. To make this clear, let me recall to you the strong human impulse which Friedrich Nietzsche (whom you despise) denominated "the will to power." This will to power is more than a mere emotion or idea, for it exists in practically every man, even the most degraded, and the mere fact that a man" makes some effort to keep alive shows that he possesses it. It is, indeed, the primal life instinct, which Arthur Schopenhauer, long before Nietzsche was born, called "the will to live."

But how does this "will to power" or "will to live" manifest itself? In civilized human societies, I believe, it shows itself chiefly in a sort of constant emulation and rivalry, which, beginning, as a lowly effort to exchange the minimum of muscular effort for the maximum of food, expands, higher up, into the complex and powerful thing called ambition. That is to say, there lies, deep down in the soul of every man who deserves to be regarded as human, an irresistible and neverfailing impulse to sell his energy and ability as dearly as he can. The more he gets in payment, the more consideration and comforts he will enjoy, and the more desirable his position will appear when compared to the condition of other men. Herein we perceive Nietzsche's reason for changing Schopenhauer's "will to live" into "will to power," for he saw clearly that the only way a man may accurately measure his success in this effort is by observing the extent of his mastery of his environment—which includes, as one of its principal factors, his fellow-men. No matter how slight the degree of a man's victory over the natural and social forces which work for his destruction or enslavement, he is to that extent the superior of the man who has been destroyed or enslaved. It is the constant effort of every man to gain such victories—to increase his comparative safety and importance. Even the saint whose cult is self-sacrifice has a yearning to be, to some appreciable extent, more sacrificing than his rival on the next pillar. Even the Pope, at the very pinnacle of human eminence, would be glad, no doubt, to exchange places with an archangel.

Well, you will find, on looking into the matter, that the average workingman has before him two practicable methods for satisfying his will to power. By the first method he enters into a conspiracy with other workingmen which has for its object an artificial "bulling" of the market wherein their skill is sold. That is to say, they endeavor to raise the market value of their skill without offering any corresponding improvement in its quality. By the second method, the individual workman seeks so to improve his own skill that it shall bring more than the average price.

The second method would seem to be the more attractive, for experience shows that it frequently has the result of lifting the man who adopts it out of the ranks of workingmen altogether, since a man who is wise enough to sacrifice imminent ease for permanent benefit is a man of forethought, and forethought is a quality so valuable and so rare that its possessor rises in the world almost automatically. But as a matter of fact, comparatively few workmen adopt this method of making secure their livelihood and safety. The vast majority adopt the first method. Instead of seeking to increase their efficiency, they try to force their employer (who is but the spokesman or representative of the rest of humanity) to take it for granted. In other words, they try to do as little as they can for their wages, and to do that little with the least possible expenditure of skill and attention.

The average workingman, indeed, particularly in America, is notable chiefly for his firm faith that his need for working is an intolerable evil, which has been laid upon him by diabolical taskmasters, and which he is justified in shirking as much as possible. It is his constant effort to give less energy to his work to-day than he gave to it yesterday, and he forces society to condone and even encourage this effort by a sort of permanent threat to cease working altogether. Search the whole history of trades-unionism in America, and you will find scarcely half a dozen attempts, by unions, to increase the efficiency of their members. But you will find a million attempts to penalize society for calling that efficiency in question.

And so, after a long journey, we come upon one very serious difficulty in your professor's maze of figures. He has brought forward his proofs mathematical—and he has forgotten the objections psychological. He has shown that 5,000,000 faithful and efficient workingmen could do all the work of Austria in less than two hours a day—and he has overlooked the fact that there are not 5,000,000 faithful and efficient workingmen in the country. He has, in a word, made the colossal mistake of assuming that, during one hour of work, the workingman does all the work that it is possible to do in an hour. He has made no allowance for inefficiency, for shirking, for laziness, for drunkenness, for illness. He has made no allowance for the fact that, in a large number of necessary industries, seasonal and climatic variations make long and unavoidable periods of inactivity. He has forgotten the ineradicable tendency of the workingman to go on strikes and holidays. He has wasted all of his fine logic upon a purely theoretical workman, who never was on land or sea. Putting the efficiency of this monster at 100, I think I am safe in assuming that the efficiency of the real workman of flesh and blood may be set down at fifteen. And if this is true, the professor's theoretical workday of one hour and twenty-two and a half minutes becomes a real workday of more than nine hours.

But anticipating all this, you answer in one place that, under Socialism, men will look upon work as a pleasure, and hint that the present effort to shirk will disappear. If I were convinced, my dear La Monte, that you actually held to any such belief, I would certainly not give over my scant leisure to this correspondence. As a matter of fact, you must be well aware that the traits and weaknesses which make the workman of to-day an unwilling and inefficient laborer are ingrained characteristics of all low-caste men—as plainly so, indeed, as their superstitiousness, grossness, emotional suggestibility (particularly in political matters), and fear of hell—and that no social cataclysm, however appalling, will convert them at one stroke into new beings. That they will improve in the 'course of time, I am firmly convinced, for they have improved steadily in the past, but their progress toward perfect efficiency, like their progress toward perfect knowledge, will always be behind that of the classes above them. The average workingman of to-day is a better man than Moses in at least one respect, for he is far less superstitious, but the Pasteurs of to-day are still as far ahead of him as Moses was ahead of the slaves who built the pyramids.

Herein you will discern my first and last objection to Socialism. I believe, in a word, that it overlooks certain ineradicable characteristics of the human animal, and certain immutable laws of the biological process. Going further, I believe that these characteristics and laws deserve to be fostered and obeyed rather than opposed, for to their influence we owe all that we have of progress. Every comfort that we have to-day was devised by some man who yearned to get more out of life than the men about him; every great truth that "helps us face existence bravely and confidently was unearthed by some philosopher who yearned to be honored above all other philosophers; every law that gives us safety and order was written by some law-maker who yearned to see his own notion of security and order prevail over the notions of others. Just as every micro-organism in the sea ooze fights for that pin point of space which will give it life while its fellows die, just so every man fights for that microscopic degree of superiority which gives him eminence over his fellowman—better food, a better coat, more leisure, greater honor, respect and love, and a more poignant and widespread feeling of something lacking after he is gone. You Socialists, seeing part of this dimly, talk of a "materialistic conception of history," and say Karl Marx invented it. But you are wrong, for it was invented for all time on the day that the first living cells began to fight over their first meal.

Such is the law of the survival of the fittest, and so it stands immutable. Socialism is only one of a hundred plans for ameliorating it, and since all of the others have failed, I believe that Socialism will fail too. That Antiparos whose maunderings you quote against me thought the invention of the waterwheel would turn all of the mill-slaves of Greece into gentlemen of leisure, lolling all day in ease and idleness, but Antiparos was wrong, for, like all the Greeks, he was entirely ignorant of the" laws which govern living organisms. Had he lived after Malthus, instead of thousands of years before him, he would have known that the waterwheel, by making bread cheaper, would soon decrease the death-rate and increase the birth-rate of Greece, and that this increased population, needing other things beside bread, would quickly turn the idle millers to profitable industry. This process has been repeated over and over again ever since.

You Socialists make a somewhat similar mistake. You propose to wipe out competition, with its frank acceptance of the law of natural selection, and to put co-operation in its place. By this plan, you say, life will be relieved of most of its present hazards, and every man in the world will enjoy perfect security, peace, and comfort. Well, supposing all this to be true, what will be the result? First and foremost, I believe, an enormous increase in population. Even admitting the possibility of curbing the actual birth-rate, it is apparent that the concerted efforts to put an end to the struggle for existence will, for a time at least, reduce the death-rate among what are now the lowest orders toward that of what is now the highest, and that this reduction will quickly swell the population of the world.

For a time, perhaps, things will go on serenely, for these extra people, let us assume, will all do their share of the work of the world. But soon or late, I take it, the human race will make the startling discovery that the satisfaction of human desires is limited, not only by the finiteness of human energy, but also by the finiteness of the earth in size and resources. That is to say, there will come a time when the wheat fields of the world will be too small to raise all the wheat needed by the race. And when that time comes a struggle for the wheat that they *can* raise will come with it, and your Socialist state will disappear. You may say that the same *impasse* will be reached eventually with things as they are, but a moment's reflection will show you that that is no answer at all. I am not trying to prove that this is the best of all possible worlds; I am merely trying to show you that Socialism cannot hope to change it. Whether we adopt Socialism or accept things as they are, we must come eternally upon periods of stress and storm, and during these periods the strong will prevail over the weak, and every manmade law that seeks to stay them will be swept away.

This happened after the French Revolution, as you yourself point out. You seem to think that the fact constitutes a criticism of my argument, but in reality it supports me. The French Revolution, as you know, had its seed back in the Middle Ages, when certain citizens of France, by reason of their superior intelligence and craft, began to acquire a vast power over the rest of the population. The sons of these medieval lords of the soil maintained their supremacy after them, and it was maintained by so many succeeding generations that, after awhile, it came to be regarded as a matter of course. Even after the race of barons began to degenerate, no one thought of disputing their sway. Meanwhile, they kept going downhill, and by the beginning of the eighteenth century they were a race of incompetent, helpless parasites, whose power over the masses rested, not upon any superiority of their own, but upon the eternal fact that the common people are ever thick of wit, ever long-suffering, and ever slow to advocate a change. The aristocracy of France was so inefficient in the time of Louis XIV that the peasants of France might have overthrown it with ease, but it took a long series of outrages and the urging of many men to make them act, and so it was not until the reign of Louis XVI that they declared open war.

Well, this old race of overlords proved an easy foe, and the victorious commoners, staggered by their almost instantaneous conquest, at once jumped to the conclusion that there was no such thing as aristocracy—that because this one had turned out to be a hollow sham, *all* were shams. The immediate result was the grotesque mob-rule of the few months following the murder of Louis XVI. Here was an actual experiment in Socialism, for all advantages of birth, wealth, and rank were swept away. Every citizen of France was the equal of every other citizen, and each was expected to serve the state according to his particular talents and training.

Well, did this mob-rule last? Not at all! It was soon found that a populace, as a populace, could no more govern itself than a drunken man could drag himself home, or a sober man could pull his own teeth. Strong men were needed to make laws and enforce them, to deal with matters above the comprehension of the rabble, to decide between parties and factions—and in a very short while these strong men began to move toward the top, while the weak went back to their old station underfoot. In place of the artificial aristocracy of strong men's great-grandsons, there arose a new and actual aristocracy of strong men. In the end, the strongest of them lorded it over all France, and nearly all of Europe.

Napoleon Bonaparte, under the influence of the old order of things, tried to perpetuate his supremacy in his descendants, but here he overlooked a new idea which had come into the world. That idea was this: that an aristocracy must constantly justify its existence. In other words, there must be no artificial conversion of its present strength into perpetual rights. The way must be always open for the admission of strong men from the lower orders, and the way must be always open, too, for the automatic expulsion of men whose strength fails. Our governmental hierarchy, here in the United States, partially satisfies this description of a sound aristocracy. That is to say, it is a despotism so long as it rules at all, but it must constantly prove its right to rule. Some day in the future, I am convinced, there will arise a man—strong enough to hold the supreme power as long as he lives, just as Senor Diaz seems likely to do in Mexico at present. In the department of commercial enterprise we have plenty of such men. James J. Hill, I suppose, will be able to keep his immense power until he dies, for it is unlikely that, in the course of the few years remaining to him, he will encounter a foe efficient enough to wrest it from him, but, for all his potency, he can do nothing whatever to safeguard it against the inefficiency of his descendants after he is gone.

The word aristocracy, to an American, always suggests the European nobility, with its peculiar system of titles and its peculiar privileges in the affairs of government. But there are aristocrats of many other sorts, and aristocracy, in itself, by no means presupposes a patent of nobility and a seat in the House of Lords. As a matter of fact, I have shown that these things are evidences, not of real aristocracy, but of that old, artificial aristocracy which, in some countries, has managed to survive—though always with lessened powers. The aristocrats of social rank and governmental influence are by no means omnipotent. In their own field they constitute the first estate, but in some other field they may be slaves.

The French Encyclopedists who spurred the peasants of France on to the massacre of the old nobility did the world a service by wiping out a sham, but at the same stroke they gave it a new sham to take the place of the old one. This new sham was the theory that all men were equal before the Lord. Voltaire, Diderot, and the others called themselves materialists, and I have no doubt that they were sincere in saying that they couldn't accept the absurdities of Christian theology, but all the same they accepted, whether openly or tacitly, the corner-stone of that theology, which is the doctrine that every man has a soul. Their whole philosophy, indeed, was based upon a belief in the sacredness of that soul. Every man, they argued, had a soul, and since every soul was of infinite sacredness, each one was as good as any other. Upon this they erected the theory of human equality.

These men were bold and ingenious, but, as I have tried to show in another place, they were vastly handicapped by their ignorance. They could scoff at Christianity all they pleased, but in the end they had to admit that they couldn't disprove it. This was because they lived a hundred years too soon. Had they written their books after instead of before the day of Charles Darwin, they would have been free from that anthropomorphism, which, despite their great powers of ratiocination, constantly colored their thoughts. Before Darwin it was easy enough for anyone to maintain that the fundamental Christian doctrines were incapable of proof, but it was only after his lifework gave us a wholly new view of the universe, and set men, for the first time, to exploring its mysteries in an orderly fashion, that it became possible for anyone to argue of Christianity not only that it was unreasonable, but also that it was actually impossible.

I have wandered into this reference to Christianity not by accident, but intentionally, and because it seems to me that, as schemes of civilization, Christianity and Socialism are identical. You Socialists call yourselves agnostics, but you still maintain the fundamental tenet of Christian theology, which is the notion that all men are God's children, and equal in his sight; and you still advocate the primary rule of Christian ethics, which is the command that every man shall love his neighbor as himself. My objection, then, to Socialism, is my objection to Christianity. It starts out with an incredible assumption and it ends with a command that no human being, so long as he remains a human being, can possibly obey.

That Christianity is impossible is shown by the fact that the world has never beheld a single real Christian. Even Christ himself fell short, for there is abundant proof that, whatever the degree of his love for humanity in general, he had a strong and quite human dislike of the moneychangers in the Temple, and that he gave way to this dislike and tried to do them injury. Like Christianity, Socialism suffers from this irreconcilable difference between its doctrines and the nature of man. Every human being comes into the world, indeed, with instincts which both Christianity and Socialism denounce as sinful. But as all moralists discover to their horror, soon or late, it is one thing to invent and denounce a sin, and quite another thing to destroy it.

This letter is already very long, and so there is very little space left to deal with your mass of statistics regarding surplus values and other such socialistic scarecrows. All you manage to prove is this: that under our present free competition and with our efficient machines, we Americans produce a great deal more than we can use. Well, is this to be lamented? For my part, I think not. On the contrary, it seems to me to be a good cause for congratulation, for it is indubitable proof that, in the struggle for existence, we Americans are measurably superior to certain other races. As we forge ahead in productiveness, these other races will become more and more dependent upon us for the necessities of life, and in the end they will become our serfs. That is to say, practically all of their energy will be devoted to earning the money we demand for the things they need.

You may say that this can never happen, since tariff walls and national pride will always stand in the way. If that is your answer, I advise you to go to your history books and see what becomes of national pride and tariff walls when a strong, rich nation looks about for an outlet for its over-production. If the poorer, less efficient nations do not, at once and without resistance, open their gates and begin to buy, as China has but recently done, they are forced to do so by the sword, and reduced, as security for their future complaisance, to the position of vassals, as has been the case in India. If it is true, as you say, that Germany is showing super-efficiency, I venture to predict that some day Germany will conquer England, for in England the whole social fabric has been made rotten by Christian sentimentality, with its accompanying coddling of the inefficient and parasitical.

Your proof that the profits of the United States Steel Corporation exceed the amount paid out as wages to its workmen is interesting, but far from portentous. You seem to regard the Steel Corporation as a mysterious, gigantic ogre which sucks the blood of the people, and does no public service whatever. As a matter of fact, it is no ogre at all, but a collection of quite human persons, such as you and I, and many of these persons belong to the class whose wrongs you deplore. That is to say, a great deal of the Corporation's stock is owned by its employees, who are thus doubly paid for their labor—first in wages and then in profits. No law prevents an employee from buying more stock. You yourself must admit that his wages are commonly more than sufficient to keep him alive, and that, in consequence, he should have a surplus for investment at the end of each year. Why doesn't he buy stock with it? Well, in many cases he does—but in other cases he invests his money in crayon portraits of his parents, or kegs of beer. He is, in brief, an ignorant and improvident man—and yet you weep over his wrongs.

That share of the Steel Corporation profits which goes to the very rich men—and this is the share, I have no doubt, which you regard as the worst menace to humanity—is not lost to the world forever, for these rich men, like poor men, have to die in the end, and even while they live they commonly give back, either willingly or unwillingly, most of the money they thus acquire. In a republic, it is impossible to devote much public money to those large but not immediately profitable enterprises which advance culture and civilization—such things, for instance, as the establishment of libraries and museums, the erection of monuments, the cleansing of cities, and the systematic study of the higher scientific (and particularly medical) problems. This is because the common people, and their elected representatives, being entirely ignorant of human history, see nothing in these things but idle vanities.

Well, here is where the predatory rich pay back their debt to humanity in general. They know the vast value of such enterprises, and their money goes into them. In this way the common people profit by the forced taxes they must pay to men of superior ingenuity and foresight. In this way the millions so feloniously acquired by Mr. Rockefeller paid for the Rockefeller Institute, which squared the account by giving the world a specific for cerebro-spinal meningitis. It seems to me that, before this old planet vanishes into empty air, the value of that one specific, to the human race, will be a hundred thousand times the value of all the securities a hundred Rockefellers could possibly amass in a lifetime.

You seem to fancy that the money acquired by a single rich man is value lost to the race in general for all time. Nothing could be more erroneous. The millions of Mr. Carnegie are going back to the public even while he lives, and a hundred years hence, perhaps, there will not be a single rich man of his blood in the world. When George Washington died he was the richest man in the New World, and yet to-day the head of the Washington clan is a small-fry druggist in a one-horse country town. The whole clan, indeed, has been so quickly absorbed into the commonalty that few Americans have ever even heard of this man.

Such is the law of evolution, which works backward as well as forward, for in order that one may gain, another must lose. Say what you will against it, you must at least admit that it has worked for human progress. And say what you will against it, you can never hope to set it aside.

Wherefore, my dear La Monte, I must again decline your courteous invitation to call you comrade.

Sincerely,
MENCKEN.

LA MONTE'S THIRD LETTER

My Dear Mencken:

I was very glad to receive your entertaining letter, and hasten to congratulate you on your complete freedom from that weakness of small minds —consistency. But I regret to see that you are growing old before your time. When Tennyson was your age he

> dipt into the future, far as human eye could see,
> Saw the Vision of the world, and all the wonders that would be;
>
> Saw the heavens fill with commerce, argosies of magic sails;
> Pilots of the purple twilight, dropping down with costly bales;
>
> Heard the heavens fill with shouting, and there rain'd a ghastly dew
> From the nations' airy navies grappling in the central blue;
>
> Far along the world-wide whisper of the south- wind rushing warm;
> With the standards of the peoples plunging through the thunder storm;
>
> Till the war-drum throbb'd no longer, and the battle-flags were furl'd
> In the Parliament of man, the Federation of the world.
>
> There the common sense of most shall hold a fretful realm in awe,
> And the kindly earth shall slumber, lapt in universal law.

There you have the sublime optimism that is the glory of the youthful mind. It was not until forty-four years later in his extreme old age that Tennyson allowed himself to be frightened by the Malthusian bogey of over-population which so perturbs your soul, and even then he himself half suspected that the change of view was due to his fastcoming dotage, "for," he tells us,

——doubtless I am old, and think gray thoughts, for I am gray;
After all the stormy changes shall we find a changeless May?

After madness, after massacre, Jacobinism and Jacquerie,
Some diviner force to guide us thro' the days I shall not see?

When the schemes and all the systems, kingdoms and republics fall,
Something kindlier, higher, holier—all for each and each for all?

All the full-brain, half-brain races, led by Justice, Love, and Truth;
All the millions one at length with all the visions of my youth?

All diseases quench'd by Science, no man halt, or deaf, or blind,
Stronger ever born of weaker, lustier body, larger mind?

Earth at last a warless world, a single race, a single tongue—
I have seen her far away—for is not Earth as yet so young?—

Every tiger madness muzzled, every serpent passion kill'd,
Every grim ravine a garden, every blazing desert till'd,

Robed in universal harvest up to either pole she smiles,
Universal ocean softly washing all her warless isles.

Warless? when her tens are thousands, and her thousands millions, then—
All her harvest all too narrow—who can fancy warless men?

Warless? war will die out late then. Will it ever? late or soon?
Can it, till this outworn earth be dead as yon dead earth, the moon?

But, in spite of your nightmare of over-population, and your fear that we Socialists in our blindness will "reduce the death-rate among what are now the lowest orders toward that of what is now the highest, and that this reduction will quickly swell the population of the world," you lavish the most extravagant eulogy upon the scientists and their capitalist patrons for discoveries that make possible just this very reduction of the death-rate at which you stand aghast! "The work that Pasteur did in the world," you tell us, "put the clock of time ahead a hundred years, and conferred a permanent and constantly cumulative benefit upon the whole human race, freeman and slave alike, now and forevermore." Your conscience evidently troubled you over the mildness of this praise, for in your second letter you went it one better by telling us that the Rockefeller Institute had squared Mr. Rockefeller's account with mankind "by giving the world a specific for cerebro-spinal meningitis. It seems to me," you add, "that, before this old planet vanishes into empty air, the value of that one specific, to the human race, will be a hundred thousand times the value of all the securities a hundred Rockefellers could possibly amass in a lifetime."

Were yours a smaller nature—and therefore more cursed with consistency—I would expect to find you using your influence with that Senor Diaz, who, you tell us, is one day to be our Dictator, to induce him to punish with death any doctor who should give to the rabble the benefit of any of these discoveries. But, knowing you as I do, I know that in spite of all your invective hurled at the mob you would be the first to put your hand into your pocket to help a poor printer threatened with rabies to get to the nearest Pasteur Institute.

Speaking of Pasteur reminds me of your fear that after two generations of Socialism there will be no more Pasteurs. How many boys who might develop into Pasteurs ever get the chance to? By good luck the wealthy Cimabue chanced to come along and look over the shoulder of the poor little shepherd lad, Giotto, and see the picture of a sheep the lad had drawn on a stone. Cimabue took Giotto to Florence, and Giotto's paintings still delight the race. How many Giottos, do you suppose, have drawn pictures equally good that no Cimabue chanced to see? I still fail to understand what you meant by your startling assertion that

Pasteurs would fail us. It must be that you think a bitter struggle for bare existence necessary to the development of talent or genius, or that you think the necessary productive work that will be demanded of every one in the future will prevent the devotion of the necessary time to science.

In regard to the first point, Lester F. Ward, who is the only sociologist America has produced (except the late Lewis H. Morgan) whom Continental scholars quote with respect, in his "Applied Sociology" tells us that "about eleven times as many talented persons belong to the wealthy or well-to-do classes as to the poor or laboring classes, although the latter are about five times as numerous as the former. The chances of success for the same degree of talent are fifty-five for the former class to one for the latter. The extremes, of course, are very much greater, and for absolute poverty or uninterrupted labor at long hours the chance of success is necessarily zero, no matter how great may be the native talent or even genius. Indigence is an effective bar to achievement. On the other hand, the resources of society may be enormously increased by abolishing poverty, by reducing the hours of labor, and by making all its members comfortable and secure in their economic relations. Any sacrifice that society might make in securing these ends would be many times repaid by the actual contributions that the few really talented among the hundreds of thousands thus benefited would make to the social welfare. For talent is distributed all through this great mass in the same proportions as it exists in the much smaller wellto-do or wealthy class, and the only reason why the latter contribute more is because their economic condition affords them opportunity."[7, 8]

---

7   "Applied Sociology", Lester F. Ward, p. 228.

8   This calculation of Lester Ward's is based on data taken from Professor A. Odin's monumental work, "Genkse des Grands Hommes," Paris, 1895. See especially Vol. I. p.529.

As examples of talented persons who did not have to struggle for an existence, he names Tasso, Petrarch, Boccaccio, Cervantes, Dante, Chaucer, Hegel, Fichte, Kant, Buckle, Bacon, Milton, Hobbes, Galileo, Adam Smith, Harvey, Darwin, Newton, Descartes, Byron, Shelley, Macaulay, Comte, Herbert Spencer, Gibbon, Disraeli, Robert Browning, John Ruskin, Victor Hugo, and many others."[9]

In regard to the second point, an hour or two of productive labor will keep our savants in the pink of physical condition for their intellectual labors, and their experiences of real, practical life will make their studies far more fruitful for humanity.

Is your bogey of over-population any more substantial than a phantom? I will not say positively that it is not; but I do say confidently that that bridge is so far ahead that we need not be preparing to cross it now. What reason have I for saying that this is an extremely remote danger? Compare the number of offspring a single pair of codfish are responsible for in a year with the number a single pair of rabbits bestow upon the earth in a like time; and then compare the rabbit from this point of view with the higher apes br the elephants or man. What do you find? Is it not that the higher the type, the lower the rate of increase? Again compare different races and classes of men. Do you not find that highly civilized countries such as France have extremely low birth-rates? If you will go to the Antipodes, where the average standard of comfort is the highest in the world, you will find a birth-rate almost as low as that of France. I well remember that Mr. Kelley, the able editor of the New Zealand *Times*, was as much of an alarmist on this subject as our own Roosevelt, and seldom let a day go by without an editorial warning on the subject, but his warnings were in vain, for the people were far too comfortable

---

9   Ward takes this list from "Genius, Fame, and the Comparison of Races," by Charles H. Cooley. Annals of the Am. Acad. Pol. and Soc. Science, Philadelphia. Vol. IX. May, 1897, pp. 317-358.

to breed as prolificly as Irish and Hungarian peasants. The historical fact, my dear Mencken, is that comfort and education decrease the birth-rate. Socialism will give comfort and education to all. Surely, you can draw the conclusion for yourself.

Chemistry and intensive agriculture promise to enable us to defy Malthus by an almost unlimited multiplication of the food supply. And Mr. Gifford Pinchot, in a speech recently reported in the Sun, told of an amount of preventable waste now going on so vast, that if we should stop it, it is difficult to say how enormous would be our increased capacity for sustaining population.

I have so many things that I want to say to you, that I grudge every bit of space and time given to commenting on your arguments. But I must note in passing your assumption that because many Austrian workingmen now are drunken, lazy, and inefficient, therefore Professor Hertzka's hypothetical 5,000,000 in the future would suffer from the same vices. Do you really think they would? What hope for the future has the average Austrian workingman now? What inducement has he to be anything but lazy and drunken? What gives me my firm and unshakeable faith in his high potentialities as an efficient worker in the future, is the very fact that he has sense and manhood enough to be discontented with the conditions under which he works now, and his laziness, inefficiency, and drunkenness are the very best possible proofs of that discontent, so pregnant with hope for humanity.

Your statement that I despise Friedrich Nietzsche can scarcely be called ingenuous, and it pains me because I am sure you cannot be ignorant that in the *International Socialist Review* for July, 1908, I, writing as a Socialist to Socialists, said:

"I do not see how any of us can help feeling that Nietzsche, the magnificently assured prophet of BEYOND-MAN, is *our* Comrade, though we cannot but grieve that his ideal included a vast mass of suffering and exploited humanity, a 'herd' or 'rabble' over which his beyond-men were to reign in glory and dionysian joy."

I submit that this is scarcely the language of contempt.

You say that we Socialists "propose to wipe out competition," and later on in the same letter you admit that Mr. Hill has so effectually wiped out competition in the railway business, that "he will be able to keep his immense power until he dies." How are we Socialists to destroy that which Capitalism has already destroyed?

I cannot allow to pass unchallenged your statement that we Socialists "still advocate the primary rule of Christian ethics, which is the command that every man shall love his neighbor as himself." On the contrary we know only too well that the only practical ethics in a society based on the production of goods for profit are the tooth, fang, and claw ethics of the jungle. You have but strengthened the Socialist argument by showing that even Christ himself could not practise the Golden Rule. We know that ethics are relative and changing, that every stage of economic development has its own code of ethics, and we are revolutionists because we believe the Social Revolution will lay the economic foundation on which all men will practise the Golden Rule as naturally and with as little thought of duty as they now breathe.

I am sorry that I should once more have to repeat that I have never made any moral argument against the existence of surplus-value *per se*. I did not represent the "Steel Corporation as a mysterious, gigantic ogre which sucks the blood of the people, and does no public service whatever." But I did prove right up to the hilt from their own figures that after every bit of what you and Mallock would call "ability" had been paid for at the highest market rates, the profits from ownership alone were far in excess of the wages for both muscle and "ability," and that this excess of production over purchasing power as represented by wages made a Social Revolution inevitable.

But now that you have suggested it I am entirely willing to admit that drawing profit from ownership without service rendered may be called, with perfect propriety, "sucking the blood of the people."

I can scarcely restrain a smile when you tell me that all is well with the Steel Trust employees because they are given the opportunity to become minority stock-holders in the Trust. Ask those who were minority stock-holders in the Erie Railroad when Jay Gould got control of it what this privilege is worth? Or, if that is ancient history, ask those who were minority stock-holders in the Chicago and Alton when it was captured by Harriman. If one fact stands out above another in modern financial history it is that stock companies are the most efficient means ever devised to transfer the savings of the middle and working classes to the pockets of the lords of finance.

When you say that rich men in the long run pay back to the community all the wealth they have drawn from it, you do not bear in mind that the great bulk of real wealth has to be reproduced every year. It cannot be paid back "in the long run." Its physical nature forbids it. Moreover, intelligent workingmen (which is merely another way of saying Socialists or Revolutionists) do not ask or expect rich men to give or pay them back anything, but they are irrevocably determined to prevent rich men or any men in the future from taking from them the lion's share of the wealth that their labor produces and reproduces every year.

What vast wealth in practice consists of are certain legal papers that give their holders the power to compel other men to work for them; and in the case of fortunes such as those of the Astors and the Vanderbilts and the great landlords of England this power is handed down from generation to generation, so that no sane man looks forward to the day when the head of the Rockefeller clan shall be nothing more than "a small-fry druggist in a one-horse country town"—unless perchance that is the occupation he happens to prefer in the Co-operative

Commonwealth, and in that case I think I am safe in promising you that no Socialist shall say him, Nay.

I hope you will pardon me for saying that I have thus far written nothing in this letter that need have been written had you read my former letters more carefully. And now I would gladly enter more fruitful fields, but, alas, I cannot yet do so, for I have not yet touched upon your gracious intimation that you would refuse to give over your scant leisure to this correspondence if you were convinced that I actually believed that "under Socialism" (by the way, Socialism is not an umbrella or an awning) "men will look upon work as a pleasure," and that "the present effort to shirk will disappear."

Much as I should regret to see this correspondence cut short (and I would regret it most deeply), I am compelled to assure you that I do most sanguinely expect work to become a pleasure, nay, I hold that all work that has been worth the doing has always given pleasure to the worker, and I do expect that the worker in the days when "all shall be better than well "will fear the imputation" of shirking even more than most women do to-day the imputation of unchastity. But, in spite of my firm faith that work of the right kind should give a normal being pleasure, I am wholly willing to concede with William Morris that "whatever pleasure there is in some work, there is certainly some pain in all work, the beast-like pain of stirring up our slumbering energies to action, the beast-like dread of change when things are pretty well with us." And here I am going to depart from my regular custom and ask you to do a little reading for yourself. I am sure you will get a far better comprehension of the Socialist point of view on this subject of work from reading William Morris's Lecture on "Useful Work *versus* Useless Toil" than it is possible for me to give you in the limits of a letter. You will find this lecture in the volume entitled "Signs of Change," published by Longmans, Green & Company.

William Morris discriminates between "two kinds of work—

one good, the other bad, one not far removed from a blessing, a lightening of life; the other a mere curse, a burden to life.

"What is the difference between them, then? This: one has hope in it, the other has not. It is manly to do one kind of work, and manly also to refuse to do the other.

"What is the nature of the hope which, when it is present in work, makes it worth doing?

"It is threefold, I think—hope of rest, hope of product, hope of pleasure in the work itself; and hope of these also in some abundance and of good quality; rest enough and good enough to be worth having; product worth having by one who is neither a fool nor an ascetic; pleasure enough for all for us to be conscious of it while we are at work; not a mere habit, the loss of which we shall feel as a fidgety man feels the loss of the bit of string he fidgets with."

William Morris anticipated that the idea of pleasure in work would come as a shock to men like yourself, for he added:

> "The hope of pleasure in the work itself, how strange that hope must seem to some of my readers—to most of them. Yet I think that to all living things there is a pleasure in the exercise of their energies, and that even beasts rejoice in being lithe and swift and strong. But a man at work, making something which he feels will exist because he is working at it and wills it, is exercising the energies of his mind and soul as well as of his body. Memory and imagination help him as he works. Not only his own thoughts, but the thoughts of the men of past ages guide his hands; and, as a part of the human race, he creates. If we work thus we shall be men, and our days will be happy and eventful."

I rejoice with you in the conquests of Science over Nature, but I hold with Morris that "Nature will not be finally conquered till our work becomes a part of the pleasure of our lives." And I hold with Morris that "if there be any work which cannot be made other than repulsive, either by the shortness of its duration or the intermittency of its recurrence, or by the sense of special and peculiar usefulness (and therefore honor) in the mind of the man who performs it freely,—if there be any work which cannot be but a torment to the worker," it were better to "leave it undone." "The produce of such work cannot be worth the price of it."

But you go on to say that I "must be well aware that the traits and weaknesses which make the workman of to-day an unwilling and inefficient laborer are ingrained characteristics of all lowcaste men." I am aware of nothing of the kind; what I am aware of is that all men in a state of nature have an almost ineradicable hatred of toil without hope, and that in what you would call highcaste men this hatred is never wholly rooted out, but that in what you would call lowcaste men centuries and centuries of discipline have made even hopeless toil a habit, the loss of which they "feel as a fidgety man feels the loss of the bit of string he fidgets with."

It is precisely among the working class (whom you describe as "lowcaste men") that work for work's sake has become a true nervous disease, and the great task before us is to cure the proletariat of its diseased and depraved appetite for work.

The free citizens of Greece and Rome in the days of their glory had a most healthy hatred for work. "I could not affirm," says Herodotus, "whether the Greeks derived from the Egyptians the contempt which they have for work, because I find the same contempt established among the Thracians, the Scythians, the Persians, the Lydians; in a word, because among most barbarians, those who learn mechanical arts and even their children are regarded as the meanest of their citizens. All the Greeks have been nurtured in this principle, particularly the Lacedaemonians."

"Nature," said Plato in his noble "Republic" (Book V), "has made no shoemaker nor smith. Such occupations degrade the people who exercise them. Vile mercenaries, nameless wretches, who are by their very condition excluded from political rights. As for the merchants accustomed to lying and deceiving, they will be allowed in the city only as a necessary evil. The citizen who shall have degraded himself by the commerce of the shop shall be prosecuted for this offense. If he is convicted, he shall be condemned to a year in prison; the punishment shall be doubled for each repeated offense."

In his "Economics" Xenophon writes, "The people who give themselves up to manual labor are never promoted to public offices, and with good reason. The greater part of them, condemned to be seated the whole day long, some even to endure the heat of the fire continually, cannot fail to be changed in body, and it is almost inevitable that the mind be affected."

"What honorable thing can come out of a shop?" asks Cicero. "What can commerce produce in the way of honor? Everything called shop is unworthy an honorable man. Merchants can gain no profit without lying, and what is more shameful than falsehood? Again, we must regard as something base and vile the trade of those who sell their toil and industry, for whoever gives his labor for money sells himself and puts himself in the rank of slaves."

There is no use in multiplying these quotations, which Paul La fargue has collected from the classics, to show you that just those traits which you regard as the special attributes of lowcaste men were in fact the characteristic traits of highcaste men in ancient Greece and Rome, just as they are in Europe and America to-day.

But I deny the validity of "highcaste" and "lowcaste" as divisions of humanity. I recognize not highcaste men and lowcaste men, but men who have had a chance to live human lives, and men who have been condemned to live the lives of beasts. If the term "lowcaste" can properly be applied to any human beings it is surely to those pitiable members of the upper classes who have been so cut off from all contact with the masses of humanity that in their breasts the broad human sympathies, the sense of human fellowship and solidarity, of racial oneness, have atrophied and died out until in their relations with all mankind outside their narrow social circles they are able to obey the great command of your master, Nietzsche, **"Be Hard!"**

I have no doubt that you would classify the private soldiers in the Italian Army as "lowcaste men." Let us judge them by their actions. Right after the Messina Earthquake the New York *Sun* sent its London correspondent to the scene, and his letter (the best piece of newspaper work I have ever seen) appeared in the issue of January 17, 1909.

"I stopped for half an hour on Monday afternoon," he writes, "to watch the dramatic climax of a rescue operation which had been going on for forty-eight hours. It was in the ruins piled forty feet high adjoining the principal theater in Garibaldi street. On Saturday morning a faint response was heard deep down in the débris to the constant cry of the rescue parties, 'Is any one there?' The original building had been a very solid one of six stories of stone and mortar. Its destruction had been as complete as if a rock the size of a house had been dropped upon it from the sky and then rolled away. It seemed impossible that anything could remain alive beneath that apparently solid mass of pulverized walls, blocks of granite, and a few splinters of wood.

"But the cry was human and fifty men set to work. They dug valiantly for hours above where the voice came. They seemed to get no nearer and night came. Searchlights were brought and the work went on. On Sunday morning the location of the sufferer was fixed more definitely. They could talk with him, and he told them he was not much hurt, there were a few inches of space about his head, and his hands were free. He pleaded not so much for release as for drink and food. The dust was suffocating and he feared he would choke if they came closer. The soldiers forced a pipe down through the debris and the imprisoned man succeeded in reaching the end of it. Beef tea and brandy were poured down in succession.

"The gratitude that came in response was as heartfelt as if the poor fellow was already in the free light and air instead of crushed down beneath twenty feet of ruins. That additional twenty feet amid material impossible to excavate by ordinary methods required another thirty hours to conquer. The impalpable powder which filled every crevice of the more solid material slipped back almost as fast as it was taken out. Besides, it was necessary to proceed with the utmost caution for the victim's sake. It was just as the rescuers had come in sight of the poor fellow that I happened to climb over that section of débris. A few moments apparently would effect his release, and a stretcher was hastily brought to the entrance of a little tunnel which had been driven through the side of the excavation. And then, when safety was in sight, the treacherous sides of the great hole began to slip, and in a few seconds the man was buried anew. There was a cry of horror on all sides. A dozen soldiers buried their faces in their hands and wept. The downpour of powdered lime and stones stopped for a moment. Suddenly the officer in charge cried:

"'Who will go in with this rope and fasten it beneath his arms underneath the dirt? It may mean death, for if the dust comes down again it will mean suffocation for whoever goes?'

"'Let me go! Let me go! I don't mind what happens to me!' were the cries from almost every man in the detachment.

"A noose was quickly made in a stout rope and a lithe young private went quickly into the bottom of that suffocating funnel. He dug away with his hands around the head of the victim. He found, fortunately, that a small arch had protected him from the worst of the last dust slide. In a few moments the rope was fixed and a dozen men dragged the poor creatures into freedom."

If those soldiers were "lowcaste" men, then so were Jesus Christ and Saint Francis of Assisi.

It is but too obvious, my dear Mencken, that you cherish what Dr. Lester F. Ward calls "the great sullen stubborn error, so universal and ingrained as to constitute a world view, that the difference between the upper and lower classes of society is due to a difference in their intellectual capacity, something existing in the nature of things, something preordained and inherently inevitable."[10]

On page 100 of the same work he tells us:

"The essential fact, however, is that there is no valid reason why not only the other partially emerged eight-tenths but the completely submerged tenth should not completely emerge. They are all equally capable of it. This does not at all imply that all men are equal intellectually. It only insists that intellectual inequality is common to all classes, and is as great among the members of the completely emerged tenth as it is between that class and the completely submerged tenth. Or, to state it more clearly, if the individuals who constitute the intelligent class at any time or place had been surrounded from their birth by exactly the same conditions that have surrounded the lowest stratum of society, they would inevitably have found themselves in that stratum; and if an equal number taken at random of the lowest stratum of society had been surrounded from their birth by exactly the same conditions by which the intelligent class has been surrounded, they would in fact have constituted the intelligent class instead of the particular individuals who happen actually to constitute it. In other words, class distinctions in society are wholly artificial, depend entirely on environing conditions, and are in no sense due to differences in native capacity. Differences in native capacity exist, and are as great as they have ever been pictured, but they exist in all classes alike."

"The proposition that the lower classes of society are the intellectual equals of the upper classes," he says in another place, "will probably shock most minds. At least it will be almost unanimously rejected as false. Yet I do not hesitate to maintain and defend it as an abstract proposition."[11]

Ferdinand Lassalle long ago pointed out that the upper

---

10   "Applied Sociology", Lester F. Ward, p. 96.

11   "Applied Sociology", Lester F. Ward, p. 95.

classes in order to defend their class privileges were obliged to oppose human progress. It is true that, here and there, there shines out like a beacon-light on the tragic pages of human history the name of a truly noble noble who rose above his petty class interests and gave his life and talents freely to humanity; but it is but too true that the majority of the upper classes in all times have been led, consciously sometimes, but far more often unconsciously, by their class interests to oppose the forward march of humanity. Fortunately for those whom you describe as "lowcaste men" they are free from this demoralizing influence, for, to quote Lassalle, "the working class is the last and outside of all, the disinterested class of the community, which sets up and can set up no further exclusive condition, either legal or actual, neither nobility nor landed possessions nor the possession of capital, which it could make into a new *privilege* and force upon the arrangements of society.

"We are *all* workingmen in so far as we have even the *will* to make ourselves useful in any way to the community.

"This working class in whose heart therefore no germ of a new privilege is contained, is for this very reason synonymous with the *whole human race*. Its interest is in truth the interest of the *whole of humanity*, its freedom is the freedom of humanity itself, and its domination is the domination of *all*.

"Whoever therefore invokes the idea of the working class as the ruling principle of society, in the sense in which I have explained it to you, does not put forth a cry that divides and separates the classes of society. On the contrary, he utters a cry of *reconciliation*, a cry which embraces the whole of the community, a cry for doing away with all the contradictions in every circle of society, a cry of *union* in which all should join who do not wish for privileges, and the oppression of the people by privileged classes; a cry of **love** which, having once gone up from the heart of the people, will *forever remain the* *true cry of the people*, and whose meaning will make it still a *cry of love*, even when it sounds the war cry of the people."

Weismann pointed out the biological reasons for the socio-logical facts stated by Lester F. Ward in the passages I have quot-ed when he tried to show that acquired characteristics were not inherited, but Weismann's theories have always been disputed, though unquestionably the majority of modern scientists have inclined to agree with him. But it was left for Gregor Mendel to establish by proof almost as clear as a demonstration in Euclid that the characteristics, talents, aptitudes, and graces acquired by education and environment cannot be transmitted by heredity. But, as Mendel was both an Austrian and a Christian monk, I shall expect you to give but scant attention to the remarkable re-sults of his biological studies. At any rate I shall not prolong this letter to tell you more about him here.

In my next letter I may tell you more about him, and I shall certainly admit your charge that Socialists are prone to accept evidence and theories that tend to help their side of the argu-ment, and I shall show you that this peculiarity is not confined to Socialists, and I shall draw some interesting deductions from these facts.

In closing permit me to commend to your prayerful consid-eration the following excerpt from the editorial columns of the esteemed Boston *Transcript*:

"Whatever the outcome of the Socialist movement in this country, ill-considered opinions on the subject are likely to be less frequent in the future than they have been. President Roosevelt, according to an apparently well authenticated story, recently wrote a paper on Socialism, severely arraigning what he supposed to be its fundamental propositions. His article was submitted for criticism to two sociologists, neither of them pro-[1] fessed Socialists, as it happened, but both conversant with the literature of the subject. So adverse was their judgment regard-ing the Presidential effort that Mr. Roosevelt tore it up, against the time when he could more thoroughly investigate the actual status of present-day Socialist doctrine."

While I know that you greatly admire Mr. Roosevelt for his insistent and incessant preaching of the Nietzschean doctrine of the strenuous life, I sincerely trust that in this instance you will not permit yourself to be tempted to follow his illustrious example.

Ever,
LA MONTE.

MENCKEN'S REPLY TO LA MONTE'S THIRD LETTER

My Dear La Monte:

Your letter, like the book of Leviticus, deals with a multitude of subjects, and I cannot hope to make a comprehensive reply to all the propositions it lays down. In this emergency I shall have to adopt the method known to professors of wrestling as catch-as-catch-can. That is to say, I shall begin at the beginning and proceed, as gracefully as possible, to the end; maintaining, all the while, a careful look-out, and dealing, from time to time, deft wallops at such of your arguments, theories, and ideas as may appear to stand in greatest need of chastisement and controversion.

At the very start you accuse me of a violent, and even vile, inconsistency, and by all the rules of evidence, in such cases made and provided, you also convict me. But I shall show you, I believe (and if you have ever sat in a court of justice and listened to its endless comedy, you will scarcely need this proof), that the rules of evidence have nothing whatever to do with the laws of logic and common sense.

Specifically, you make allegation that I have been blowing both hot and cold. In one place, you point out, I maintain that a sudden and rapid increase of population, among the lower orders, would be a menace to human progress; and in some other place

I pay eloquent tribute to Pasteur and his ilk, whose delving into culture-tubes has reduced the death-rate of all orders, high and low. On the face of the thing, I seem to argue here, (a) that it is well to let the ape-men die; and (b) that we should encourage pathologists to save them. But this seeming, my dear La Monte, is only seeming.

Your error lies in your neglect of the vast difference between an increase in population in which the lowest caste makes the greatest strides, and an increase in population in which, if there is any relative advantage at all, the highest caste enjoys it. It is an increase of the first sort that would appear if all the wealth in the world to-day were distributed among the loafers and incompetents. But it is an increase of the second sort that appears when the doctors happen upon some new antitoxin, vaccine, rule of clean living or health resort.

It must be plain to you, I am sure, that the epoch-making medical discoveries of the last halfcentury have benefited the lowest caste far less than they have benefited the highest caste. If you have never given the matter thought, just consider, for a moment, the case of tuberculosis. Fifty years ago the mortality in this wide-spread disease, among all who developed the secondary symptoms, high and low, rich and poor alike, was probably not far from sixty per cent. To-day, among intelligent persons of the higher castes, the mortality is not much above twenty per cent.; but among the lowest caste of negroes and foreigners it is still well over fifty per cent.

And why? The ready answer is that the treatment of tuberculosis is a tedious and exceedingly expensive business, and that those patients who are poor and friendless must perforce die. This is a fair enough answer, so far as it goes, but it does not go very far. In place of it I wish to offer another answer, and it is this: that the majority of persons who succumb to preventable and curable diseases to-day go down to their graves, not so much because they are poor, as because they are ignorant—because they are handicapped by the low-caste man's chronic and ineradicable suspiciousness, orthodoxy, stupidity, lack of foresight, and inability to learn.

My own city of Baltimore, on account of its wealth of hospitals and clinics, has been called the medical capital of the New World. Its hospitals are open to all, and those who cannot pay are given treatment free. It is possible for a man without a cent in his pocket to profit by the skill of the greatest physicians and surgeons in America. Beyond the city boundaries are free sanitoria for the treatment of tuberculosis and other infectious diseases. Medicines and nursing are free. Those too ill to move are treated and nursed in their homes. The attentions for which visitors from all parts of the country pay thousands of dollars are free to every indigent citizen. And yet the death-rate of Baltimore is higher than that of any other city of its size in the United States.

The Christian Scientists, of course, say that this is because there are so many hospitals, but the real reason lies in the fact that among Baltimore's 600,000 inhabitants there are 100,000 negroes and 200,000 ignorant and superstitious foreigners. The negroes, when they grow ill, take patent medicines or send for some frowsy quack of their own race. When they grow worse, they summon a filthy black ecclesiastic and begin to pray to God. The result is that the death-rate among the lowest classes of these semi-human savages is fully sixty per thousand per annum. This is just about five times the normal death-rate among civilized white men.

Is the negro—or low-caste white man—to blame for his poverty and ignorance? No more, I think, than he is to blame for his filthiness and dishonesty. He can't help being lazy and he can't help being stupid, for he is a low-caste man, and he has a low-caste mind. That mind is unable to grasp any but the most elemental concepts. Tell him, as his pastors tell him, that if he gives five cents to the church he will be saved from hell, and he can understand it. But try to make him grasp the complicated chains of ratiocination whereby civilized man has determined that vaccination will almost infallibly prevent smallpox and rabies, that quinine will cure malaria, and that a long and complex treatment will arrest tuberculosis—and he is as pitifully helpless as the average college professor in the presence of a problem not solved in the textbooks.

I think you perceive, by now, that I do not regard Pasteur and his fellow-explorers as saviours of the great masses. Their work, true enough, has perceptibly alleviated the sufferings of even the lowest castes, but its chief value, by long odds, has been to the higher castes. It is only, indeed, by reason of the despotic intimidation of these higher castes—an intimidation, it may be said, which always has its chief spring in notions of self-defense—that the lower castes have been compelled, willy nilly, to enjoy any benefit at all. We vaccinate negroes, not because they want to be vaccinated or because we harbor a yearning to preserve their useless lives, but because we don't want them to fall ill of smallpox in our kitchens and stables, and so expose us to inconvenience, danger, and expense. With few exceptions, they are piously opposed to baring their arms, and regard the necessity for so doing as proof positive that they are down-trodden and oppressed. Let them choose for themselves, and they would be dying of smallpox to-day just as copiously as they are dying of tuberculosis.

In their vain rebellion against the very things which make life bearable for them, they reveal the eternal philosophy of the low-caste man. He is forever down-trodden and oppressed. He is forever opposed to a surrender of his immemorial superstitions, prejudices, swinishness, and inertia. He is forever certain that, if only some god would lend him a hand and give him his just rights, he would be rich, happy, and care-free. And he is forever and utterly wrong.

I am glad you made necessary all this explanation of my apparent inconsistency, for it gives me a chance to explain another matter in which you probably misunderstand me. The thing I refer to may be best indicated, perhaps, by the question, what factors determine the caste of a man? You Socialists are prone to assume that all who stand without your ranks subscribe to what you call the capitalistic or bourgeois theory of civilization, and I have no doubt that you regard me as one of its advocates. That is to say, you probably believe that I judge a man's importance by his material success in life—that I look upon all poor men as men of low caste, *ipso facto*, and all millionaires, nobles, and governmental functionaries as men of high caste. But that is by no means true.

As a matter of fact, the standards I should like to set up are far more complicated than this bourgeois test. They admit many a relatively poor man to the highest of all castes, and they place many a very rich man in that nadir caste which offers a refuge for the congenital idiot, the scrofulous, the faith-curist, and the believer in signs, hunches and St. Anthony of Padua. They are standards, as I have said, of a certain complexity, and if, at times, they seem to admit one and the same man to both a very high caste and a very low one, I have only to urge in their defense that human existence is a very complex and puzzling thing, and that I have no faith whatever in the socialistic idea that it will be possible, some day, to solve all of its riddles with one master-equation.

Well, then, what virtues do I demand in the man who claims enrollment in the highest caste? Briefly, I demand that he possess, to an unusual and striking degree, all of those qualities, or most of them, which most obviously distinguish the average man from the average baboon. If you look into the matter, you will find that the chief of these qualities is a sort of restless impatience with things as they are—a sort of insatiable desire to help along the evolutionary process. The man who possesses this quality is ceaselessly eager to increase and fortify his mastery of his environment. He has a vast curiosity and a vast passion for solving the problems it unfolds before him. His happiness lies in the consciousness that he has made some progress to-day in comprehending and turning to his uses those forces which menaced him yesterday. His eye is fixed, not upon heaven, but upon earth; not upon eternity, but upon to-morrow. He enters the world infinitely superior to a mere brute, and when he leaves it his superiority may be expressed (in bad algebra) by infinity plus x. By his life and labors, the human race, or some part of it, makes some measurable progress, however small, upward from the ape.

You will observe that this fine frenzy for improvement, for change, for progress, is entirely absent in even the highest of the lower animals. It is also absent, perhaps, in the very lowest types of human beings; but here, at least, it certainly begins to appear far down the scale. The most ignorant and miserable slave in central Asia is able, I take it, to formulate some idea of a state of being preferable to his own; just as the most degraded American negro is equal to the concept of a land flowing with milk and honey. But here we begin to note a distinction which differentiates the merely sentient man from the unmistakably higher man. The one dreams chaotic dreams, without working out practicable plans for their realization. The other, having efficiency as well as imagination, makes the thing itself arise out of the idea of it. The one pins his faith to Christianity, Socialism, or some other vaporous miracle-cult. The other peers through microscopes, builds great steamships, reclaims deserts, makes laws, and overturns the gods.

And so I arrive at my definition of the firstcaste man. He is one whose work in the world increases, to some measurable extent, that ever-widening gap which separates civilized man from the protozoon in the sea ooze. It is possible, you will note, for a man to amass billions, and yet lend no hand in this progress; and it is possible, again, for a man to live in poverty, and yet set the clock ahead a thousand years. It is possible, once more, for a man to aid progress in one way and aid reaction in some other way. And so, to sum up, it is possible for a poor man to belong to the highest caste of men, and for a rich man to belong to the lowest; and it is possible, again, for one and the same man to belong, at different times or even at the same time, to both castes. If you think this last idea an absurdity, let me cite John D. Rockefeller as an example. His vast improvements in the interchange of commodities entitle him to a place in the front rank of those whose lives have made for human progress; and yet his belief, as a good Baptist, that total immersion in water is a necessary prerequisite for entry into heaven, places him, quite unmistakably, in the lowest caste of superstitious barbarians.

Now, what I want to insist upon, in all this, is that the distinction I have described is the product, not so much of varying environment as of inborn differences. I admit freely enough that, by careful breeding, supervision of environment and education, extending over many generations, it might be possible to make an appreciable improvement in the stock of the American negro, for example, but I must maintain that this enterprise would be a ridiculous waste of energy, for there is a highcaste white stock ready to hand, and it is inconceivable that the negro stock, however carefully it might be nurtured, could ever even remotely approach it. The educated negro of to-day is a failure, not because he meets insuperable difficulties in life, but because he is a negro. His brain is not fitted for the higher forms of mental effort; his ideals, no matter how laboriously he is trained and sheltered, remain those of the clown. He is, in brief, a low-caste man, to the manner born, and he will remain inert and inefficient until fifty generations of him have lived in civilization. And even then, the superior white race will be fifty generations ahead of him.

I have used the negro as an example because in him the inherited marks of the low-caste man are peculiarly conspicuous. In some of the European peasants who are now coming to America—and particularly in those from Russia—the same marks are to be seen. These peasants differ as much from the highcaste white man as a mustang differs from a Kentucky stallion, and this difference is the product, not of their actual environment, but of their forefathers' environment through innumerable generations. They represent a step in the ladder of evolution below that of the civilized white man, and no conceivable change of environment could lift them to the top *en masse*, in a lifetime. Individuals of extraordinary capacity occasionally appear among them—the naturalists call such abnormal individuals "sports"—and pass over automatically and at once into some higher caste. But they can get no higher than a caste in which individuals fully equal to them are the rule instead of the exception; and the generality of their race must forever remain below.

Castes are not made by man, but by nature. They will be inevitable so long as every genus of living beings in the world is divided into species, and every species is made up of individuals whose resemblance to one another, however close it may be, never reaches identity. It is this variation which makes progress possible, for it gives certain individuals an advantage in the struggle for existence, and these individuals tend to crowd out their weaker brothers, and to make their own heartier qualities dominant in the general racial strain. Among the lower animals the struggle for existence is frankly a matter of dog eat dog. Among men, it is more elusive, and the alert, curious, intelligent man I have described has an even greater advantage, perhaps, than the man of mere physical vigor. But whether the weapons in the struggle be sharp teeth or efficient brains, there must always be a caste of victors and a caste of vanquished. Any effort to suspend the struggle is empty vanity—and I here use the word in both of its common meanings.

But Professor Ward dissents. He holds that "class distinctions in society are wholly artificial, depend entirely upon environing conditions, and are in no sense due to differences in native capacity." At first sight this sentence seems to be an unqualified denial of the law of natural selection—a thesis, I fancy, that not even a Socialist would care to maintain—but, as a matter of fact, Professor Ward is merely trying to argue that congenital differences, while actually existing, are counterbalanced by class privileges and vested rights. In other words, he believes that a man's place in the world is determined, not by the intelligence and capacity he brings into the world, but by the fortuitous circumstances, opportunities, and surroundings he encounters after his arrival. A man with the intellect of a Huxley, born to a family of Baptist farm laborers, may remain ignorant, superstitious, and degraded until the end of his days. And a man but a hair's breadth removed from imbecility, born to a noble house, may square the circle or change the map of the world.

This theory, as I have before indicated, is the favorite fallacy and chief solace of all degenerate and inefficient races of men. "If I had a million dollars"—but you know the rest of it as well as I. It is one of the multitude of sophistries that meet the pragmatic test of truth, for it plainly makes life more bearable. The man who formulates it enjoys a comforting glow of relief, of conscious virtue, of martyrdom. He has found a scapegoat to bear the blame for his inability to rise above the morass in which he wallows, and that scapegoat he variously denominates fate, luck, civilization, plutocracy, privilege, the protective tariff, civil service reform, or the devil.

If, as the pragmatists and supernaturalists would have us believe, the mere persistence and agreeableness of an idea were proofs of its truth, this one would be perpetually and indubitably true. But I cannot bring myself to accept so ingenuous a gnosiology. As a matter of fact, I am firmly convinced that the idea we are discussing tends to become, not true, but false, in exact ratio to its persistence and agreeableness. That is to say, in the case of a man to whom it occurs but occasionally and then only in moments of emotional weakness, it may be true very often. But in the case of the man who adopts it as his working philosophy of life, it is not true more than once in ten million times.

The efficient man of highest caste makes it his rule to accept the world as he finds it, and to work out his own salvation with a light heart. His joy is in effort, in work, in progress. A difficulty overcome, a riddle solved, an enemy vanquished, a fact proved, an error destroyed—in such things he finds the meaning of life and surcease from its sorrows. But the inefficient man, unable by his own hand and brain to cope with the conditions J which beset and menace him, seeks refuge, soon or late, in the notion that the world is out of joint. Sometimes he concludes, finally, that the horrors of existence are irremediable, and then he is ripe for religion, with its promises of repayment in some gaseous paradise beyond the grave. At other times he arrives at the idea that all would be well if there were some abysmal reconstruction of the scheme of things—some new deal of the cards, with four aces pushed his way. When this madness falls upon him he gropes about for a ready guide to the Utopia that arises nebulously in his brain. And thus it is that discontented, ignorant, helpless men subscribe to the poetical fancies of imaginative dreamers, and become single-taxers, Christian Scientists, Anarchists, or Socialists.

The great objections to Socialism, as a philosophy, are that it encourages and aggravates the feeling of martyrdom which burns in the breasts of all such incompetents, and that it inflames them, at the same time, with the idea that their discomfort is due, not to the operation of natural laws, which benefit the world by ridding it automatically and harshly of the unfit, but to the deliberate and devilish cruelty of their betters. Your true Socialist is firmly convinced, before everything else, that his personal existence is of vast and undoubted value to the world, and that the world, if it were not a swindling felon, would reward him handsomely for remaining alive.

Now, since the majority of all Socialists belong to the laboring class, and get their living by joining their muscle-power to the natural forces which man has harnessed—because of this circumstance, the general idea I have set forth is transformed, by Socialists, into the specific doctrine that the only truly valuable man is the "producer." That is to say, the only human service which fully earns and deserves the reward provided by the law of supply and demand, is that sort of service which results in the production of some commodity necessary to the actual day-to-day existence of mankind. Such a service deserves, not some definite reward, but *all* the reward that those who require it may be bludgeoned into paying for it. Thus the farmer who hoes a cabbage patch, and by taking advantage of the hunger of his fellow-men, makes them pay for his cabbages, is, by the socialistic philosophy, a virtuous man. His fellow-men have less cabbages than they need and the farmer himself has more than he needs. Very well, then, let them pay his price! But the man who has a surplus of some other valuable thing, say shrewdness, capital, forethought, intelligence, or cunning, and demands a fair profit on the exchange from those who have less than they need, and desire to buy of him—this man, by the socialistic philosophy, is a criminal.

You Socialists, my dear La Monte, here overlook the fact that no man worthy of the name is content to stand still. He wants to be richer, more learned or more powerful to-morrow than he was yesterday. In other words, he looks, not only for a fair equivalent, but also for a profit, in all of his exchanges with his fellow-men. Your laboring brothers are demanding that profit to-day. They want, not only fair wages, but the whole value of the things they produce. Well, the same selfish weakness afflicts their masters, too. The latter, when they buy muscle-power, want enough to balance the money they pay for it—and a profit beside. The laboring man has nothing to give except muscle-power, and so, after he has given enough of it to balance his pay, he must give a little more to make up his master's profit. As I have told you in the past, I think you greatly exaggerate the actual percentage of profit, in all such transactions; but that there always is a profit, and a distinctly appreciable one, I admit very readily. If there were none at all, no efficient, highcaste man would engage in industrial enterprises; for no man of that sort could possibly rest content with standing still.

Sincerely,
MENCKEN.

LA MONTE'S FOURTH LETTER

Dear Mencken:

I must apologize for some slight delay in answering your last very interesting letter. The fact is that your great and good friend, Mr. Roosevelt, did not take the advice of his sociological friends and destroy his anti-socialist manuscripts, but instead unloaded them on the *Outlook*, with the result that on the very day I had set apart to write to you I received a hurry-up call for a reply to that eminent Nietzschean, our ex-President.

And now, when I should be planting potatoes and peas, I must devote a few hours to your enlightenment, but my little encounter with Mr. Roosevelt has vastly increased my respect for you. In your three letters thus far you have not made as many blunders as Mr. Roosevelt perpetrated in the first *Outlook* article alone, and you have never shown a tithe of the bitterness.

After reading your letter there arose in my mind a picture of you which, had I the pencil of a Ryan Walker or a McCutcheon, I should draw for you. In this picture you are hotly pursued by hostile and malevolent Socialists, and seeing no escape elsewhere you have sought rescue and shelter by throwing yourself into the arms of a good old Baltimore colored "mammy." Really, this picture has so captivated my imagination that I have not the heart at once to tear you from her protecting arms. For the present, I shall content myself by warning you that even there you are not safe from the terrible Socialists.

I should never have guessed from the appearance of the Baltimore darky that he (or she) was the Palladium of our sacred institutions. But, in the language of Bernard Shaw, "You never can tell." This important role has, by most critics of Socialism, been forced upon that humble and useful person, the scavenger.

"I have seldom," says Robert Blatchford in "Merrie England," "heard an argument or read an adverse letter or speech against the claims of justice in social matters, but our friend the scavenger played a prominent part therein. Truly this scavenger is a most important person. Yet one would not suppose that the whole cosmic scheme revolved on him as on an axis; one would not imagine him to be the keystone of European society—at least his appearance and his wages would not justify such an assumption. But I begin to believe that the fear of the scavenger is really the source and fountain head, the life and blood and breath of all conservatism. Good old scavenger! His ash-pan is the bulwark of capitalism, and his besom the standard around which rally the pride and the culture and the opulence of British society."

Poor old scavenger! His occupation has gone; you have given his job of "saving society" to the Baltimore darky.

But we shall return to the "colored man and brother" later. At present I want to express my gratification at having at last discovered what you mean by your favorite phrase, "high-caste men." It is now obvious to me that the perfect type of your first-caste man is the Christian priest or clergyman.

You say that his distinguishing characteristic is "a sort of insatiable desire to help along the evolutionary process." In other words he shows primitive animistic habits of thought by exhibiting what I described in "Socialism: Positive and Negative"[12] as "the tendency to give a teleological interpretation to evolution, to attribute a meliorative trend to the cosmic process, as in Tennyson's 'through the ages one. increasing purpose runs.'"

---

12   page 97

That this cropping out of a semi-theological habit of thought in your last letter is not a mere fortuitous phrase, but is on the contrary part and parcel of your habitual view of the universe, is shown by your statement in your first letter that your "creed consists, first and last, in a firm belief in the beneficence and permanence of the evolutionary process."

Thorstein Veblen has this to say of the origin of this habit of attributing ethical purposes or effects to "natural laws":

> "Along with the habits of thought peculiar to the technology of handicraft, modern science also took over and assimilated much of the institutional preconceptions of the era of handicraft and petty trade. The 'natural laws,' with the formulation of which this early modern science is occupied, are "the rules governing natural 'uniformities of sequence,' and they punctiliously formulate the due procedure of any given cause creatively working out the achievement of a given effect, very much as the craft rules sagaciously specified the due routine for turning out a staple article of merchantable goods. But these 'natural laws' of science are also felt to have something of that integrity and prescriptive moral force that belongs to the principles of the system of 'natural rights' which the era of handicraft has contributed to the institutional scheme of later times. The natural laws were not only held to be true to fact, but they were also felt to be right and good. They were looked upon as intrinsically meritorious and beneficent, and were held to carry a sanction of their own. This habit of uncritically imputing merit and equity to the 'natural laws' of science continued in force through much of the nineteenth century; very much as the habitual acceptance of the principles of 'natural rights' has held on by force of tradition long after the exigencies of experience out of which these 'rights' sprang ceased to shape men's habits of life. This traditional attitude of submissive approval toward the 'natural laws' of science has not yet been wholly lost, even among the scientists of the passing generation, many of whom have uncritically invested these 'laws' with a prescriptive rectitude and excellence; but so far, at least, has this animus progressed toward

disuse *that it is now chiefly a matter for expatiation in the pulpit, the accredited vent for the exudation of effete matter from the cultural organism."* [13]

You, my dear Mencken, do not appear to be yet wholly free from anthropomorphic habits of thought, as it is obvious you give the clergy no inconsiderable aid in their onerous task of exuding effete matter from the cultural organism.

My own ideal man would be a man wholly devoted to promoting *human* happiness (and mind I have said human happiness, not a hog's conception of happiness), and who would be entirely prepared, in case it should be necessary to achieve his goal, to strive manfully to modify, avert, or defeat the 'natural' results of the evolutionary process. The man who feels "a sort of insatiable desire to help along the evolutionary process" is still fast enmeshed in the bonds of superstition, and has merely made a fetish of "the evolutionary process" to erect upon the altar from which he has hurled the old gods.

If the hypotheses of Mr. Percival Lowell in his recent brilliant book on Mars are correct, the "evolutionary process" there, had it not been modified and interfered with by intelligence, would by this time have almost wholly exterminated both vegetable and animal life on that interesting planet. But whether his hypotheses be right or wrong, this illustration will enable you to conceive that circumstances may arise that will make the opposing of the "evolutionary process" the highest function of the "high-caste man."

But, although it would be difficult to find many educated and intelligent men to-day outside the ranks of the clergy who could give in an unqualified allegiance to your creed—the creed of your "men of the first caste"—I know well enough that it is not your belief that the whole scheme of things should be shaped

---

13   Thorstein Veblen. "The Evolution of the Scientific Point of View." University of California Chronicle, Vol. X, pp. 413-414.

with a view to producing the maximum number of clergymen. For you, indeed, increase of the priesthood is synonymous with retrogression.

By "high-caste men" you really mean men of intelligence and energy—truly emancipated men, and if the increase of such men is to produce the effects you expect, you must also impute to them kindly emotions.

But will not your "high-caste man" of the future be terribly lonesome amid the "rabble"? Without insulting the good people of Baltimore, may I ask if you do not at times feel impelled to imitate Bernard Shaw's Eugene Marchbanks in "Candida " and talk to yourself out loud? "That is what all poets do," Marchbanks said, "they talk to themselves out loud; and the world overhears them. But it's horribly lonely not to hear someone else talk sometimes."

That remark pierces the fundamental weak spot" in your ideal and Nietzsche's; could you realize fully your ideal to-morrow, loneliness would turn, your paradise for Supermen into a veritable hell.

Any ideal that does not include the closest possible approximation to economic equality suffers from this same vice. Without economic equality, you may mitigate but you cannot eradicate the hell of loneliness which to-day makes discontented persons of you and me and hosts of others. "A wholly emancipated person," says Lester F. Ward, "finds himself almost completely alone in the" world. There is not one perhaps in a whole city in which he lives with whom he can converse five minutes, because the moment anyone begins to talk he reveals the fact that his mind is a bundle of errors, of false conceits, of superstitions, and of prejudices that render him utterly uninteresting. The great majority are running off after some popular fad. Of course the most have already abrogated their reasoning powers entirely by accepting some creed. The few that have begun to doubt their creed are looking for another. They may think they are progressing, but their credulity is as complete as ever, and they are utterly devoid of any knowledge by which to test the credibility of their beliefs."[14]

And here we come back for a minute or two to the "colored man and brother." As long as you are compelled to live in the same city with some thousands of negroes, whom you appear to find more or less uninteresting as fellow-citizens, would it not be wise to see if by increased opportunities they might not be made more interesting? If poverty-stricken, drunken negroes spreading vermin and syphilis and other contagion throughout your city are, as they undoubtedly are, a perpetual menace to your peace and happiness, would it not be wise to make a brave and honest attempt to free the negroes from poverty and syphilis and drunkenness? Would not Baltimore then be a pleasanter city in which to dwell?

Unless you have the courage to go to the Nietzschean extreme and boldly advocate the extermination of the negro (and the Russian peasant, whom you place in the same category) you must join the Socialists in their efforts to enable the negroes to live human lives under human conditions. For the people of Baltimore this is merely a question of self-defense or rather selfpreservation.

To demand for the negro a chance to live a truly human life is not to assert his equality in all respects with the white race. Says Enrico Ferri, "Socialism says: *Men are unequal, but they are all men.*

"And, in fact, although each individual is born and develops in a fashion more or less different from that of all other individuals,—just as there are not in a forest two leaves identically alike, so in the whole world there are not two men in all respects equals, the one of the other,—nevertheless every man, simply because he is a *human being*, has a right to the existence of a man, and not of a slave or a beast of burden."[15]

---

14   "Applied Sociology," Lester F. Ward (Boston, 1906) p. 81.

15   "Socialism and Modern Science," Enrico Ferri (New York, 1904) pp. 20, 21.

But as a matter of fact up to the present time negroes as a race have enjoyed so few opportunities that it is utterly unscientific to dogmatize about their potentialities. It is just as unwarranted to deny their potential future equality as it is to deny their present inequality.

Lester F. Ward, after reviewing the evidence for and against racial inequality, sums up the matter as follows:

"It is not therefore proved that intellectual inequality, which can be safely predicated of all classes in the white race, in the yellow race, or in the black race, each taken by itself, cannot also be predicated of all races taken together, and it is still more clear that there is no race and no class of human beings who are incapable of assimilating the social achievement of mankind and of profitably employing the social heritage."[16]

That is all that Socialism demands for the negro, and the South will never be a desirable place of residence till that demand is granted.

That is my honest belief, and I probably imbibed in my youth as much prejudice on the negro question as you did, for I passed three years at a Southern boarding school and at the University of Virginia.

In closing my last letter, I promised in this to admit your charge that Socialists are prone to accept evidence and theories that tend to help their side of the argument, and to show you that this peculiarity was not confined to Socialists, and to draw some deductions of importance from these facts.

The fact is that all beliefs that have been held by considerable bodies of people have been begotten by desires, and that these desires are the emotional expressions of economic interests. Although I would not blame you if you should be growing weary

---

16   "Applied Sociology," Lester F. Ward, (Boston, 1906), p. 110.

of my frequent quotations from Lester F. Ward, I cannot refrain from quoting his admirable exposition of this point.

"It may be said," he writes, "that the universal world ideas which are said to lead or rule the world are simply beliefs. This is very nearly true, and therefore we need to inquire specially into the nature of beliefs. The difference between belief and opinion is slight, at least in popular usage. Belief might be defined as fixed or settled opinion, but there is also embraced in it a certain disregard of the evidence upon which it rests, while in opinion a certain amount of evidence is implied. Opinions admit of comparison as regards their strength depending upon the evidence, and may be very feebly held, the 'weight' of evidence in their favor being nearly balanced by that against them. This cannot be said of beliefs. In these the evidence is not thought of. They are absolute and independent of all proof. Upon what, then, do they rest? Here we reach the kernel of our problem. *Beliefs rest on interest.* But what is interest? It is *feeling.* World views grow out of feelings. They are the bulwarks of race safety. You cannot argue men out of them. They are the conditions to group as well as to individual salvation.

"Now it is just this element of interest that links beliefs to desires and reconciles the ideological and economic interpretations of history; for economics, by its very definition of value, is based on desires and their satisfaction. Every belief embodies a desire, or rather a great mass of desires. In this lies the secret of its power to produce effects. The belief or idea, considered as a purely intellectual phenomenon, is not a force. The force lies in the desire. And here we must be careful not to invert the terms. The belief does not *cause* the desire. The reverse is much nearer the truth. Desires are economic demands arising out of the nature of man and the conditions of existence. They are demands for satisfaction, and the sum total of the influences, internal and external, acting upon a group or an individual, leads to the conclusion, belief, or idea that a certain proposition is true. That proposition, though always reducible to the indicative form, is essentially an imperative, and prompts certain actions regarded as essential to the preservation of the individual or the group. The fact that the interests involved are sometimes transcendental interests and become increasingly so with the intellectual development of the race, does not affect the truth of all this. All interest is essentially economic, and seen in their true light religious interests are as completely economic as the so-called material interests. All conduct enjoined by religion—not only the most primitive but also the most highly developed religions—aims at the satisfaction of desire, of which the avoidance of punishment is only a form, for economic considerations are always both positive and negative in this sense. And if in the higher religions the positive interests come to predominate over the negative ones, this only renders them more typically economic in their character."[17]

This idea that religious ideals have economic roots cannot be unfamiliar to such a student of Friedrich Nietzsche as yourself. Do you not recall that wonderful passage in "A Genealogy of Morals" in which he tells us how *ideals are manufactured* on earth? He shows how the early converts to Christianity, being weak and slaves and helpless, falsified "weakness into *desert*," and "impotence which requiteth not into 'goodness'; timorous meanness into 'humility,'" and called "not-to-be-able-to-take-revenge" "not-to-will-revenge, perhaps even forgiveness."

But while the idea that religious beliefs have been moulded by economic conditions is familiar to you, you will probably be startled when I assert that this is equally true of scientific beliefs. I developed this thesis very inadequately in a paper on "Science and Revolution" in the *Social-Democrat* (London) for March 15, 1909, and after I had mailed the manuscript I received from Professor Veblen a copy of his paper on "The Evolution of the Scientific Point of View" (from which I have already quoted in this

---

17   "Applied Sociology," Lester F. Ward, (Boston, 1906), pp. 45-46

letter), which develops the same thesis with far greater clearness and ability.

In the former paper I wrote:

> I have no disposition to deny the essential truth of Modern Science and the great potential benefits it has conferred upon humanity, when I assert that the form of scientific theories has been largely determined by the economic conditions amid which they arose, and that—this is the important point—their acceptance by large bodies of adherents has depended upon their fitness to meet the desires—desires produced by economic needs—of those adherents.

This general position was assumed by Karl Kautsky in his "Social Revolution," and, with more facts at his disposal, Arthur Morrow Lewis has elaborated it still further in his lecture on De Vries' "Mutation" in his excellent little handbook "Evolution: Social and Organic" (Chicago, 1908); but even since those books were written the development of scientific theory has overwhelmingly reënforced the view that science responds to economic stimuli.

Space will not permit me to give here any save the briefest sketch of scientific theory during the last century and a quarter.

When the bourgeoisie were fresh from their revolutionary conflict with feudalism—the great French Revolution—and were still extending their dominion, they were iconoclastic and revolutionary in spirit. It was precisely then that the cataclysmic theories of Cuvier in geology and biology became the generally accepted theories of science. Cuvier accounted for the existence of fossil remains of animals different from any living species by assuming that from time to time in the past great cataclysms (earthquakes and eruptions) had occurred and wiped out all living forms of life, and that fresh creations had filled the vacancies. This theory at the same time accounted for the conformation of the earth's surface. The same cataclysms had dug oceans and lakes and piled up mountains.

Contemporary with Cuvier was Lamarck, and Lamarck proclaimed the true theory that animals had descended from ancestors unlike themselves, but there was no large class of people to whom this doctrine was acceptable, and Lamarck died disgraced, and Cuvier in the height of his glory was called upon to pronounce his eulogy, and took advantage of the opportunity to malign him.

By the middle of the nineteenth century, the bourgeoisie were firmly seated in the saddle; the last vestige of feudalism and the restrictions of the guild system (and in England of protective tariffs) had been wiped out; the bourgeoisie had the proletariat just where they wanted them. In a word, they had no more use for revolutionary theories in their business; if changes must come, let them come a step at a time. Thus the conditions for the wide acceptance of evolutionary theories in biology and geology were ripe, so that in spite of the rage of the clergy nothing could prevent the general conquest of the scientific world by the natural selection of Darwin and Wallace, and the uniformitarian geology of Sir Charles Lyell. So true is this that on last Friday (February 12, 1909), the centenary of the births of Abraham Lincoln and Charles Darwin, many of the clergy who had been called upon to deliver Lincoln orations were unable to restrain themselves from adding a word of tribute to Charles Darwin.

Darwin, like Lamarck, taught that animals had descended from ancestors unlike themselves, and that the changes in animals leading to new species had been very slow and gradual. It is true that Darwin and Lamarck differed as to the means by which these changes had been brought about, but in the particulars I have named they were at one. Yet Lamarck was dishonored, and to-day most men look upon Darwin as the greatest genius of the nineteenth century. Why this difference? Economic conditions is the only possible answer.

Sir Charles Lyell laid great stress upon the minute changes in the earth's surface that are always in progress, and reduced the rôle of cataclysms to an extremely insignificant one—and he became the recognized father of modern geology. Sir Charles Lyell taught us much and valuable truth; the small changes he noted are actually constantly going on, and their accumulated effects are tremendous, and before Lyell's day they had been unnoticed and neglected. But his great reputation raised to a sacred dogma the utterly indefensible doctrine that (to translate the pedantic Latin) "Nature makes no leaps."

Darwin taught that natural selection seizes upon the minutest variation that gives the individual even the slightest imaginable advantage in the struggle for existence, and that the fixing and accumulation of these infinitesimal variations in time brings about the introduction of new species. At the very time when Darwin was pursuing his researches, the laws of heredity were being experimentally worked out in a monastery garden in Brünn, Austria, by a monk who had previously studied natural science in Vienna. This monk was Gregor Mendel, the discoverer and formulator of the laws of heredity. His studies have enabled us to predict mathematically the results of almost any conceivable experiment in hybridization. Incidentally, his studies showed that slight variations in height, etc., that might be of marked advantage to the individual in whom they occurred, were no more likely to appear again in his progeny than they were in the progeny of less favored individuals. The remarkable results of Mendel's studies were published in the "Proceedings of the Natural History Society of Brünn" in 1865, just six years after the publication of Darwin's famous "Origin of Species." It is only fair to note that, so far as we know, Darwin never knew anything of the work of Mendel. But the important point for us is that there was at that time, as it were, no market for the discovery that the raw material for natural selection to work upon must consist of "leaps" or, in other words, of much more marked and considerable variations than Darwin and Wallace had worked so hard to prove the adequacy of. And the fact is that Mendel's remarkable paper was forgotten and buried, and was not exhumed and resurrected until the dawn of the twentieth century by some earnest scientific workers at the University of Cambridge.

What had happened in the meantime to bring about a readiness in the minds of large bodies of intelligent men and women to accept cataclysmic theories in the natural sciences? There can be but one answer—the appearance of the ever-growing International Social Democracy. Economic conditions had created an army of 30,000,000 or 40,000,000 earnest men and women steadfastly striving for revolution, and among them were to be numbered the cream of the intellectuals of both hemispheres. Here was the "demand" for cataclysmic theories, and with the closing decade of the nineteenth century science began to furnish the "supply." This supply is now increasing so rapidly that the task of keeping abreast of the new theories is bewildering, and the danger appears to be that by the close of this, the first decade of the twentieth century, our most advanced scientists will be teaching that nature makes nothing but leaps, that all development is by cataclysms or revolutions. At all events, we are reasonably sure that the charge of being unscientific will not much longer be hurled at the revolutionists in the Socialist ranks. In the second decade of the twentieth century we may expect to see the opportunists and reformers using their utmost ingenuity to answer the very charge they have so often hurled at our heads.

Toward the close of the nineteenth century a Dutch botanist, Hugo De Vries, noticed some new varieties of evening primroses in his garden near Amsterdam. They came from some self-sown plants of the common American Lamarckiana. "In the test condition of De Vries' own garden," Mr. Lewis tells us, " in an experiment covering thirteen years, he observed over fifty thousand of the Lamarckiana spread over eight generations, and of these eight hundred were mutations divided among seven new elementary species. These mutations when self-fertilized, or fertilized from plants like themselves, bred true to themselves, thus answering the test of a real species. De Vries also watched the field from which his original forms were taken, and saw that similar mutations occurred there, so that they were not in any way due to cultivation."

That was the main contribution of the nineteenth century to cataclysmic biology. De Vries held that Darwin admitted the possibility of such mutations in addition to the ordinary lesser variations or "fluctuations" which Wallace and most Darwinians have held to be the only raw material that Nature provides for natural selection to work upon, and in this he is probably correct, though it is beyond question that Darwin devoted most of his life to proving the adequacy of "fluctuations."

Mr. Punnett, of Cambridge, who is the leading exponent of Mendelism, in his book on that subject, "Mendelism"[18], says that where fluctuations appear to be inherited they are probably "in reality small mutations." He summarizes the case in this way: "Of the inheritance of mutations there is no doubt. Of the transmission of fluctuations there is no very strong evidence. It is therefore reasonable to regard the mutation as the main, if not the only, basis of evolution."

Remember, this is the extreme swing of the pendulum. He really admits that natural selection preserves some small changes, too, but he re-christens such changes "small mutations." But it would be just as fair for a revolutionist to infer from this that Nature works only by revolutions, as it ever was for an opportunist reformer to infer from Darwin's teaching that Nature works only by evolution. As a matter of fact, in neither case is there any justification for transferring a law of biology to a totally different science, sociology.

Space will not permit me to give more than a glimpse at

18   "Mendelism", Reginald Crundall Punnett, (Cambridge, 1907)

similar changes in other sciences. Professor T. J. J. See, who has been in charge of the United States Astronomical Observatory at Mare Island, near San Francisco, has made a profound study of earthquakes, and published his results in the "Proceedings of the American Philosophical Society" at Philadelphia. He has also summarized them in more popular form in the September (1908) number of the *Pacific Monthly*. His conclusion is that all mountains have been formed by earthquakes caused by the secular leakage of the ocean bottom. Is not that cataclysmic enough for you? Is it true? I do not know, but it appears to have the indorsement of such scientists as the Swedish physicist, Arrhenius, and the French astronomer, Camille Flammarion. At least, it seems beyond question that some mountains are formed in that way, so we must bid a long farewell to the old uniformitarian geology.

Astronomy has shown itself equally unable to resist the cataclysmic tendency of the day. In *Harper's Magazine* for January, 1909, Professor Robert Kennedy Duncan, of the University of Kansas, tells us that "the nebular hypothesis of Laplace is no longer tenable," that its place has been taken by the "planetesimal hypothesis" of Professor T. C. Chamberlain, of the University of Chicago. This means that astronomers now believe that our solar system has been formed, not by the infinitely slow cooling down of a vast sphere of fiery vapor, forming one ring and then one planet after another during almost an infinity of time, but by a sudden explosion in our ancestral sun which formed all our planets at once by a single cataclysmic stroke! To describe the character of their production Professor Duncan uses the word "catastrophic."

. . . It is difficult to name a branch of science in which the cataclysmic theory is not triumphant to-day.

Hegel's maxim that "Nothing is; everything is becoming" has become the fundamental assumption of all science. The chemists who have investigated the radioactive bodies have shown us one chemical element turning into another in a fashion to make rejoice the heart of an old-time alchemist. Discussing this point, M. Lucien Poincare says: "We shall have to abandon the idea so instinctively dear to us that matter is the most stable thing in the universe, and to admit, on the contrary, that all bodies whatever are a kind of explosive decomposing with extreme slowness."[19]

Let us be careful not to go to extremes and deny the fact and the fruitfulness of slow evolution, but let us with equal determination assert the necessity and efficacy of cataclysmic revolution!

You see, my dear Mencken, I freely admit that we Socialists believe in the theories and arguments making for Socialism because we *want* to believe in them, because we believe it is to our *interest* or to the interest of humanity for us to believe in them. But those who oppose Socialism do so because they believe it to their interest to do so.

I believe I have demonstrated the economic foundation of beliefs in the field in which such a foundation would have been least suspected—that of the natural sciences—so that I think we may, regard Lester Ward's view of beliefs as holding good universally.

But while the beliefs of both the friends and foes of Socialism rest on economic foundations, there is this prime difference between them:—the Socialist foundation is steadily spreading in area and growing in strength and solidity, while the anti-Socialist foundation is disintegrating and crumbling away. The pervasive influence of the Machine Process is extending ever farther and deeper and making more thoroughgoing the standardization of life, and is thus ever multiplying and invigorating the desires that make for Socialism at the same time that it is sapping the strength of the desires that stand in the way of Socialism. Unless you can point to some new force that will intervene and retard the spread of the influence of the Machine Process, you are compelled to admit that the time when the vast majority of mankind

---

19   "The New Physics," M. Lucien Poincare, (Appleton, 1908)

will be Socialists is not far distant. This is the sort of an "evolutionary process" that I and my comrades (whether you regard them as "high-caste" or "low-caste") have "a sort of insatiable desire to help along."

But though I saw plainly enough the effect of economic conditions upon scientific theory when I wrote the paper from which I have quoted so liberally, it was not until I read the illumining paper by Thorstein Veblen on "The Evolution of the Scientific Point of View" that I saw that so long as science was a mere shuttlecock tossed hither and thither by varying class interests nothing worthy of the name of science was so much as possible. Not until the Social Revolution shall have wiped out class lines forever, will a true science, that is a broadly human, instead of a class, science, arise.

Literature too awaits the vivifying breath of the Social Revolution. "Under class civilization," says Marcus Hitch, "all literature as well as all science may be called toy work; it does not make for human progress directly but only incidentally. The sciences and inventions are exploited by corporations primarily for profit, and all new discoveries merely broaden the field of exploitation and give rise to larger corporations. The toy literature and arts merely serve for the diversion of the same class; they affect the upper surface of society only and do not rise to the dignity of really human productions, because they are not participated in by humanity, nor is it intended that they should be."[20]

The same point is possibly more clearly brought out by M. Alfred Odin, Professor in the University of Sofia, in his great work, *Genèse des grand hommes, gens de lettres français moderns.*

"Literature then is not," he writes, "in its origin, and hence in its essence, that vague, ethereal, spontaneous thing whose phantom so many historians and literary critics have been pleased to evoke. It is in the full force of the term an artificial creation, since

---

20   "Faust," Goethe, (Chicago, 1908), pages 38-39

it is derived essentially from causes due to the intentional intervention of man, and has not resulted from the simple natural evolution of mankind. It is a natural phenomenon only as it faithfully reflects the inner mental workings of certain social strata. It possesses nothing "national or popular. Literature can only be national when it springs from the very bosom of the people, when it serves to express with equal ardor the interests and the passions of the whole world. French literature does not do this. With rare exceptions it is only the mouthpiece of a few privileged circles. And this explains why, in spite of so many efforts of every kind to spread it among the people, it has remained upon the whole so unattractive and so foreign to the masses. Born in the atmosphere of the hotbed it cannot bear the open air. Not until, from some cause or other, the whole population shall be brought to interest itself actively in intellectual affairs will it be possible for a truly national literature to come forth which shall become the common property of all classes of society."[21]

The same story is to be told of art as of literature and science. But this letter is already overlong, so I shall content myself by giving William Morris's reason why to-day we can have no true art. "In one word," he says, "slavery lies between us and art."

Do you wish to live to see a true science flourish? Then, become a soldier of the Social Revolution!

Do you wish to see a great human literature blossom? Then, become a soldier of the Social Revolution!

Do you wish to see all life made beautiful by noble art? Then, become a soldier of the Social Revolution!

The recruiting office is always open.

Yours, &c.,
R. R. La M.

---

21   "*Genèse des grand hommes, gens de lettres français moderns,*" M. Alfred Odin, (Paris, 1895), p. 564

MENCKEN'S REPLY TO LA MONTE'S FOURTH LETTER

My Dear La Monte:

You begin your letter by discoursing of scavengers, and I shall imitate your example. The scavenger, you point out quite accurately, is the favorite bugaboo and Exhibit A of many of the principal opponents of Socialism. They wonder who will volunteer to do the scavenging in the Socialist state, and their wonderment is soon transformed into a denial that any scavenging will be done at all. So pictured, the socialistic landscape takes on a disagreeable aspect. Heaps of garbage disfigure the highroads; there are dead cats in the reservoirs, and the Louvre is full of tomato cans. The nose cries out aloud for mercy and the human race falls prey to zymotic disease.

This seems to be the idea at the bottom of the Rev. Thomas Dixon's anti-socialist novel, "Comrades." The comrades of his socialistic island, when the time comes to choose avocations, forget entirely the daily drudgery of the world. More than half of the women want to be chorus girls, college professors, and wealthy widows, and ten per cent. of the men immolate themselves upon the altar of national banking. Not a hero asks an option on the ash-cart. Not a soul offers to look after the plumbing.

There is humor in the scene, but not a great deal of truth. As a matter of fact the scavenger is by no means the most ignoble of men, and his profession never lacks willing recruits. His social position, indeed, is palpably higher than that of the prostitute, male or female, the pickpocket or the mendicant. The undertaker, a scavenger with a touch of poetry, is a respected citizen in every American village, and even in so large a town as Philadelphia the freemen once chose an undertaker for mayor. The scavengers who have rid the Canal Zone of mosquitoes will live in history, and not many years hence their effigies will grace the public places of Colon. The trained nurse spends half of her waking hours in scavenging, and so do the doctor, the sailor, the dairyman—all honorable men. The housewife's eternal foe, so the soap advertisements tell us, is dirt. You and I are scavengers, too—you, when you apply the whisk-broom to your raiment, and I when I flick my cigar ashes out of the window, instead of behind the piano.

No, there is no prejudice against scavenging, but rather, among the fastidious, a passion for it; and so far as I have been able to observe, no very active ostracism of scavengers. The man who calls each morning to empty my garbage can is a high dignitary in the Patriotic Order Sons of America, and has ten times as much political influence as I have. On election day he ceases from his labors and devotes himself to inoculating the great masses of the plain people—of whom I have the honor to be one—with enthusiasm. At public gatherings of the electorate he bears a torch and howls like a wolf. On election day I find that he has already voted when I reach the polling-place, and I enjoy the soothing consciousness that his ballot has nullified mine. Later on, perhaps, he will vote again, for he has nothing else to do all day. As for me, I must get back to my desk and finish my article on "The Republic *versus* Despotism."

Considering all this, I agree with you that the reverend, but fanciful Dixon, and all those other critics of Socialism who hail the scavenger as their deliverer, are trusting themselves to a far from triumphant hero.

But all the same, I am forced to appear, if unwillingly and as a traitor, in the camp of these critics, for I, too, fasten an argument against Socialism upon the scavenging gentleman. My argument, however, differs materially from theirs, for while they see in Socialism a scheme of things that would annihilate him, I see in it a scheme that would elevate him to the high estate and dignity of the gods. Under our present democracy the scavenger, if he have ambition in him, may become the equal of an Edison or a Cyrus Field—on certain limited occasions and in certain limited respects. Under Socialism he would be the peer of these infinitely superior men at *all* times and in *all* respects!

In other words, Socialism is indissolubly linked with the doctrine that a man, merely by virtue of being a man, is fitted to take a hand in the adjudication of all the world's most solemn and difficult causes. It insists that the voice of the ignorant shall be heard as respectfully as the voice of the learned. It contends that the yearning of the hod-carrier for a high hat and a keg of beer shall receive as much consideration as the yearning of an Ehrlich for the secret of cancer. It maintains that the Russian-born tailor, filthy to his finger tips and the devotee of an outlandish, incomprehensible creed of nonsensical text-searching, shall be the equal of the men who conquer the wilderness and harness the lightning. It sees something portentous and holy in the trivial accident that the negro loafer, drowsing in his wallow, was born without a tail. It fastens a transcendental importance upon the word "human" and converts it into a synonym for "intelligent," "honest," "wise"—for every adjective that distinguishes" one caste of men from the caste below it. You may protest all you please, and qualify your meaning of "equality" however you please, but the fact remains that if this notion that one man is as good as another—"before God," or "as a citizen"—be taken away, Socialism ceases to be intelligible to rational creatures.

But am I arguing, I hear you ask, against government by the consent of the governed? Do I propose the overthrow of our democracy and the erection in its place of some form of absolute monarchy or oligarchy? Not at all. All things considered, I am convinced, as you are, that the republican form of government in vogue in the United States and England to-day is the best, safest, and most efficient government ever set up in the world. But its comparative safety and efficiency lie, not in the eternal truth of the somewhat florid strophes of the Declaration of Independence, but in the fact that those strophes must ever remain mere poetry. That is to say, its practice is beneficent because its theory is happily impossible. Once a year we reaffirm the doctrine that all men are free and equal. All the rest of the twelvemonth we devote our energies to proving that they are not.

It is lucky for civilization that democracy must ever remain a phantasm; to entertain and hearten the lowly like the hope of heaven, but to fall short eternally of realization. If it were actually possible to give every citizen an equal voice in the management of the world—if it were practicable to provide machinery whereby the collective will of the majority could be registered accurately, and made effective automatically and immediately—the democratic ideal would reduce itself to an absurdity in six months. There would be an end to all progress. Emotion would take the place of reason. It would be impossible to achieve coherent governmental policies. The mind of the government, as a government, would be the mind of the average citizen of the nether majority—a mind necessarily incapable of grasping the complex concepts formulated by the progressive minority. The more childish the idea the more eagerly it would be adopted and put into execution. The more unreasoning the prejudice, the more desperately it would be cherished and the longer it would survive.

An example may make this somewhat more clear. You are familiar, I suppose, with the enormous value of the work done by the national Department of Agriculture. It has multiplied our national wealth, it has reduced the labor of our farmers and increased their leisure, and it has greatly elevated our standards of living. And yet, as you know, its efforts were ridiculed and opposed by nine-tenths of the farmers in the United States when it began, and even to-day the majority of them look upon it as their officious enemy. But a few months ago, when experts went through Maryland showing the peasants how to increase the yield of their cornfields, a howl of objurgation went up.

Let us suppose that the project of establishing a Department of Agriculture had been referred to a universal manhood plebiscite, and that all the votes had been counted fairly. Do you believe that the farmers of the country, with their seven-tenths majority, would have said aye? I think not. And supposing the Department established, do you believe that a referendum would have supported it in its infinitely useful, but iconoclastic, and hence obnoxious, work? Again, I think not.

Fortunately, it is impossible, under our existing system of denaturized democracy, for the freemen of the land to record their judgment upon all the countless administrative issues that arise—or even upon the major issues of general policy. Theoretically, true enough, they determine the latter by their votes, but actually, it is always possible for the intelligent minority to drive them, buy them, or lead them by the nose. The use of brute force against the mob is a constant, but seldom recognized expedient of civilized government. A President of honesty and intelligence sacrifices his chance of re-election in order to execute some plan for the national benefit. The electors will cast him out on that impending November day, but meanwhile he has the power of the State behind him, and so his plan is put through. Again, there comes a crisis, in some division of the State, in the conflict between the intelligent minority and the lowest caste of the majority. The latter attempts to assert its god-given "rights"—to substitute barbarism for civilization. Well, the shot-gun does a solemn work—and disfranchisement appears as a footnote to the

Declaration of Independence. Marcus Brutus and the Ku Klux Klan were of a piece. In despotism it is assassination that stands between the slave and his ultimate, unbearable wrong, and in republics it is despotism that saves civilization from the slave.

The lesser weapons that I have mentioned are bribery and sophistry. You know, as well as I, how each is wielded, and you know, too, that each, in the long run, works as much good as harm. If it were not possible for politicians to hoodwink and bamboozle the electorate, the Secretary of State at Washington would practise the statecraft of the village grocery store. Luckily for all of us, the truly vital problems of government are seldom left to the decision of the majority. If, by chance, they enter into a campaign, it is always possible to drag a herring across the trail, and so send the plain people galloping after it. Their actual choosing, when it is done, narrows down to a choice between a fat man and a lean man, a platitude and a fallacy, tweedledum and tweedledee. One candidate proposes to curb the trusts, and his opponent proposes to curb the trusts." There is a noisy wrangle over identities—and the luckier of the two aspirants gets his chance. Once he is in office, the actual issues of the campaign engage him no more. Instead, he devotes his time to the execution of ideas which he has scarcely mentioned, perhaps, in his canvass, but which he knows to be of importance and value. The platitudes of the platforms have served their purpose, and no one will hear of them again until the next campaign.

Bribery, I believe, is often more efficient, in combating the eternal running amuck of the Chandala caste, than either brute force or sophistry. Certainly, it is more subtle than the former and more honorable than the latter. The minority decides what it wants and what it can afford to pay—and the majority gratefully accepts its money. In my own glorious State of Maryland fifty per cent. of the voters expect—nay, demand—to be paid for their votes. If, by any accident, there were no competitive bids on election day, it would puzzle them sorely to decide how to vote. In some of the counties, I am told, fully ninety per cent. accept honorariums from the party disbursing officers. Horrible? Not at all. Just suppose that these swine actually recorded their own thoughts in the ballot-box! Just suppose that the honest opinions of the Eastern Shore of Maryland, white and black, were transformed into laws upon the statute-books of the State! If they were, it would be a misdemeanor to call a Baptist clergyman an ass, and a felony to put a lock on a henhouse door.

And yet you Socialists, whether you are disposed to admit it or not, propose to wipe out the just and providential disabilities which now differentiate all such vermin from their betters. You tell the whining, inefficient man, with his constant cry of injustice and oppression, that he must get the things he wants through the ballot-box. "Vote for Debs," you say to him, "and you will be paid, not only your fair wage, but your employer's profit also. Vote for Debs, and you will be able to live at the rate of $5,000 a year. Vote for Debs, and your hours of labor will be cut to two a day. Vote for Debs, and the by-laws of your trades-union will become the constitution of the Republic."

Well, suppose he does it, and gets all that he now seeks. Will he be content, then, to loll contentedly in his new luxury, with his $5,000 a year, his twenty-two hours of idleness, his crayon portrait of his grandmother, his automatic piano, his diamond shirt studs, his automobile, and his half-hourly can of beer? I think not. Once he becomes the economic and political equal of his former employer he will proceed to enforce his equality, politically as well as economically. He will become, in brief, a statesman, a disputant, a philosopher—and after that, God help us! His heroes will be the men who think as he thinks. He will send the intellectual giant in the next ditch to Congress. The boss of his union will aspire to the Presidency. The secretary of the scene-shifters will go to the Court of St. James.

This picture, my dear La Monte, is not fantastic. The clodhopper's distrust of his betters will be accentuated, rather than ameliorated by Socialism. Our scavenger, even after he is the political and economic equal of Dr. Eliot and Mr. Rockefeller, will still view such men with suspicion—if there be, indeed, any men of their sort in the socialistic state—because it is an inherent and ineradicable characteristic of all low-caste men to look with suspicion upon those whose ambitions, ethics, and ideals are more complex than theirs. The old hatred of the man who would rather read a book than bask in the sun has not died out in the world. The old cry of sorcery is still raised. And the low-caste man, whenever he has the chance, still prefers to trust himself to a delegate from his own caste, whose yearnings are his, and whose mental processes he can follow. Socialism can never change this. It is a matter of anatomy more than of economics.

At the present time, when an election district peopled in overwhelming majority by low-caste men, sends one of them to a state legislature, his power for evil is obscured and neutralized by two things. In the first place, he meets few of his fellows there, for the average low-caste electoral body is so corrupt that its class-feeling is easily overcome by money, and in consequence he cannot make himself felt. In the second place, he is commonly corrupt himself. If you have any practical acquaintance with politics in any American state, you must be well aware that the legislators who are most easily purchased are those who come from the ranks of the workingmen and farmers. The bucolic statesman, when he gets to the state capital, makes his fight for the trivial local laws that his own self-interest demands, and after that he is for sale to the highest bidder. The more important matters before the law-making body are entirely beyond his comprehension. He doesn't understand them, and he doesn't want to understand them. I know, indeed, of a case wherein a large city, seeking authority from the state legislature to make improvements demanded urgently by the public safety, was unable to get that authority because it was impossible, under its charter, for it to pay certain county members for their votes. If there had been time, I have no doubt, these county members would have obligingly amended the charter to make the payments legal.

Socialism will not convert such simple barbarians into civilized men. Despite their $5,000 a year and their twenty-two hours of leisure, they will still cling to their rag-time, their yellow journals, their medicated flannels, and their fear of hell, learning, and the bath-tub. But under Socialism, you say, they will have leisure for education. Even supposing they still hold to their present custom of devoting an hour a day to pinochle, they will yet devote some other hour to John Stuart Mill and August Weismann. It is a beautiful theory, but the facts, I fear, do not point to its truth. Education, considered in its broad sense, and not as a mere piling up of special knowledge, is not a matter of leisure and money, but of inclination and capacity. It is perfectly possible in the United States to-day for the average boy, white or black, to obtain, without cost to his parents, just as much education as Herbert Spencer ever had from others from beginning to end of his life. In many states it is compulsory. But for all that, we produce very few men comparable to Spencer.

As a matter of fact, the typical low-caste man is entirely unable to acquire that power of ordered and independent reasoning which distinguishes the man of higher caste. You may, by dint of heroic endeavors, instil into him a parrotlike knowledge of certain elemental facts, and he may even make a shift to be a schoolmaster himself, but he will remain a stupid and ignorant man, none the less. More likely, you will find that he is utterly unable to assimilate even the simplest concepts. The binomial theorem is as far beyond his comprehension as an epigram in Persian. And this inability to understand the concepts formulated by others is commonly but the symptom of a more marked incapacity for formulating new concepts of his own. In the true sense, such a being cannot think. Within well-defined limits, he may be trained, just as any other sentient creature may be trained, but beyond that he cannot go.

The public school can never hope to raise him out of his caste. It can fill him to the brim—but then it must stop. He is congenitally unteachable. A year after he has left school, he has forgotten nearly all that he learnt there. At twenty-one, when the republic formally takes him into its councils, he is laboring with pick and shovel in his predestined ditch, a glad glow in his heart and a strap around his wrist to keep off rheumatism.

The barriers of caste are not artificial, my dear La Monte, but natural. Sitting in school beside the Sudra I have been discussing is a boy whose future will rise above ditches. He is from the lowest caste, too, but he is a variation, a mutation. He has a thirst for learning, and a capacity for it. He may be the Galileo of tomorrow, and then again he may be only a nascent Napoleon of ditching—a dealer in the toil of ditch-diggers. But whether his progress beyond the actual toilers be great or small, he must forever stand as a living proof that there is a caste of men higher than theirs—a caste of men more intelligent than they, and more nearly approaching the maximum of human efficiency. His superiority owes nothing to vested rights, and nothing to special privileges. It is based entirely upon the eternal biological truth that, in all the more complex varieties of living beings, there are enormous differences between individuals, and that these differences, at their extremities, produce a caste barely entitled to life and a caste far advanced upon the upward path which the species seems to follow.

The negro loafer is not a victim of restricted opportunity and oppression. There are schools for him, and there is work for him, and he disdains both. That his forty-odd years of freedom have given him too little opportunity to show his mettle is a mere theory of the chair. As a matter of fact, the negro, in the mass, seems to be going backward. The most complimentary thing that can be said of an individual of the race today is that he is as industrious and honest a man as his grandfather, who was a slave. There are exceptional negroes of intelligence and ability, I am well aware, just as there are miraculous Russian Jews who do not live in filth; but the great bulk of the race is made up of inefficients. In the biological phrase, the negro runs true to type. There are few variations, except downward. I have known, I should say, at least five hundred negroes in my time, and of all these not more than ten have displayed any inclination whatever to rise above their racial level.

Socialism, as I understand it, proposes to let these savages plunder civilization. It holds that they should get more pay for their loafing; that the comforts and luxuries which represent the ideals and ingenuity of the highest caste of human beings should be handed over, gratuitously, to these parasites. It proposes to heed and satisfy their yearnings, to take account of their opinions, to give them a hand in the government of the state, to dignify their laziness with sounding names, to hail them as brothers. I am unable, my dear La Monte, to subscribe to this scheme. I am far from a Southerner in prejudice and sympathies, though born on the borders of the South, but it seems to me that, so long as we refrain, in the case of the negro loafer, from the measures of extermination we have adopted in the case of parasites further down the scale, we are being amply and even excessively faithful to an ethical ideal which makes constant war upon expediency and common sense.

And now let me return to your letter. In one part of it, I note, you accuse me of harboring anthropomorphic ideas, and proceed to elect me a member of some Methodist synod. Herein, my ingenuous friend, you juggle with words, for you are certainly well aware of the meaning of anthropomorphism, and if you are, you are certainly well aware that my belief in "the beneficence and permanence of the evolutionary process" does not make me an anthropomorphist. But I shall assume that you are actually in error regarding the meaning of the word, and so expound it.

Anthropomorphism, then, is a name for a theological theory which assumes that the universe is managed by a definite being or beings whose mental processes and emotions are similar to those of human beings. That is to say the anthropomorphic god is merely an omnipotent and omniscient man. The Greeks believed that there was a whole race of such gods, and that they spent their time on Olympus much as the Athenians spent their time in Athens—carousing, drabbing, playing politics, fighting, intriguing, and indulging in all sorts of outbreaks of passion. The modern soldier of the Salvation Army believes there is only one god, and this god he pictures as an enlarged and gaseous simulacrum of General William Booth—as a venerable but somewhat dictatorial and revengeful old man with a white beard and a large corps of favorites and assistants. The Salvationist believes that this god manages the world just as General Booth manages the Army—rewarding the faithful, denouncing the traitor, and watching eternally for fidelity and treason.

The other anthropomorphic sects draw pictures, more or less fantastic and incredible, of other manmade gods, and there are endless differences in detail. One holds that its god sometime enters the body of an actual man—that he has done so in the past or will do so in the future. Apostolic Christianity and Mohammedanism are examples. Others hold that he elevates favored human beings to his own rank, and places them at his right hand. Of such are Mormonism and Catholicism. Yet another sect maintains that its god is a sort of glorified chief of its own race, and that all other races are inferior in consequence. This comforting doctrine is taught by Judaism.

As you will notice, the central fact in anthropomorphism is that the god is given essentially human attributes. He is not only intelligent, but also extremely emotional. He has fits of temper, passions, prejudices, even superstitions. He is bland and forgiving to those he holds in affection, and furiously vengeful upon those he dislikes. It is necessary, in order to get a favor, or even common justice from him, that he be put in a good humor—by abasing one's self before him, by making some sort of sacrifice to him, or by actually bribing him. He has hordes of spies, agents, and emissaries, who collect his fees, denounce his enemies, and manage his business. He is, in a word, an exceedingly inflammatory being, with the hot passions, arbitrary likes and dislikes, and violent rages of a medieval bishop.

Now, it seems to me that the cosmic process shows no traces at all of this human emotionalism. It is, indeed, utterly unemotional, and its lack of emotion is its principal characteristic. Since the dawn of history men have been trying to read into it some notion of right and wrong—some anthropomorphic ideal—but they have always failed. Judged by those human standards which we apply to sociological processes—the operation of the state laws, for example—it is utterly immoral and meaningless. Try as we may, we can never show that our particular god punishes the guilty and rewards the righteous, or even that he comprehends the concepts represented by these words. We may assume it, but all the evidence is against it. No Huxley was needed to point out that the weather, for one thing, is managed, humanly speaking, in an ignorant and outrageous manner. No Johan Bojer was needed to prove that the wicked often triumph in the world, and the righteous often perish. And no Joseph Conrad was needed to show us that human destiny is one with the fall of the die.

Fortunately, it is not necessary for a civilized human being of the twentieth century to believe in a man-like god. I may observe and study the workings of the universe, and still make no attempt to explain them in terms of passion and emotion. It would interest me immensely to learn how and why the globes are kept spinning, but in view of the limits which hedge in my perceptions, I doubt that I shall ever find out. Meanwhile, however, I can make note of the fact that they always spin in a certain way, and that they have done so ever since the first human observers began to study them, and from this I can deduce the not unreasonable idea that they will continue to spin in that way for a good while to come. Thus, very simply, I may arrive at my notion of the permanence of the cosmic process. And, going further, I can note that the spinning of these globes, however much it has inconvenienced and tortured individual men, from time to time, has at least resulted in the gradual development of a race which seems to me to be measurably superior, in its higher ranks, to the asexual cell from which it has sprung. And so I may come to the notion that the cosmic process, considered broadly, is beneficent. Yet I have not touched anthropomorphism, directly or indirectly, at any place.

You yourself are the anthropomorphist; not I. You still hold to the ancient theological doctrine that the human race is a race apart—that because it is molded "in the image of God" it is superior to natural laws which govern other races. In the days when men believed that Jerusalem was the capital of the universe this was a credible doctrine; but the history of all exact knowledge is the history of its gradual decay. When adventurers proved, despite St. Augustine's masterly logic, that the earth was a sphere, it received a telling blow. When they proved, despite Moses, that the earth was but one of countless worlds, it received another. And when Darwin came, and his like, it ceased to be a living doctrine, and became a mere empty shell upon the garbage-pile of dead ideas. But you Socialists want to resurrect it. You ask us all to believe it, as John the Baptist believed it—despite a mass of evidence so enormous that one man can scarcely hope to master even its daily accretions.

And so I find myself at the end of my letter with many of the arguments in your last epistle unanswered. One or two brief notes must suffice. You say in one place, for example, that your ideal man is one "wholly devoted to promoting human happiness," and then proceed to explain, with somewhat unparliamentary innuendo, that you mean "*human* happiness, and not a hog's happiness." My answer here must be the "You're another," of the small boy, for it is your scheme of things, and not mine, that considers the yearnings of the hog. My own philosophy disregards the hog entirely. Its concern is with the aims and aspirations of the higher man, and with those expedients which permit him to widen the gap which separates him from the hog. But you are for the nether swine. Their desire for forty acres and a mule, for ten hours of pinochle instead of one, for leisure to be hoggish, for a chance to plunder their betters—this desire appears to you as a holy thing. You want to strike an average between the topmost man and the hog, and to achieve a level of civilization in which intelligence and hoggishness shall be blended in equal portions. Let us have no more talk of hogs.

Your argument that the individualist must suffer agonizing loneliness demands a more extensive answer than I can give. For the present, I can only point out that you are assuming too much when you assume that solitude is inevitably painful. The low-caste man's insatiable desire for company, for fraternity, for brotherhood, is a proof of his low caste. He has no resources within himself. Save in association with his fellows he has no means of defending himself, or amusing himself. Even in his own sight, he is inconceivable save as an undifferentiated molecule in a larger mass. So he joins fraternal orders, goes to church, and affiliates with a political party. A man of greater complexity is in better case. Human intercourse is open to him when he desires it, but it is not the only thing that stands between him and unbearable ennui. When he is alone, it is because he wants to be alone, and he is not lonely.

The long argument of Lester F. Ward, that all human beliefs are grounded upon the appetites and emotions, is entirely unconvincing, and so is your dissertation in support of it. The progress of such exact sciences as astronomy and biology is due, in the main, to the fortuitous collocation (humanly speaking) of apparently disconnected observations and discoveries, and has nothing whatever to do with the food supply of the state or the political theories of the people. The discovery of the bacillus of tuberculosis was made possible by the microscope, and not by the French Revolution. As for your argument that the present age is "catastrophic" and that, in consequence, "cataclysmic" theories are dominant in all departments of science, I am unable to offer a serious answer to it, because it seems to me to be utterly gratuitous and ridiculous. What is the "cataclysmic" element in Metchnikoff's theory of phagocytes, or in Wright's theory of opsonins? What had political economy to do with Dr. Remsen's discovery of saccharin? And what had the war on the bourgeoisie to do with the rise of abdominal surgery?

I fear you are joking. If you are not, you have been sadly led astray by the sound of words.

As always,
H. L. M.

LA MONTE'S FIFTH LETTER

My Dear Mencken:

Permit me to grovel before you in apologizing for my long delay in replying to your last very interesting denunciation of the herd. The fact is my garden has absorbed my energies so completely I have had no time to write.

Much of what you say in your last letter is undeniably true. Were our legislation to become the crystallization of the cultural stage reached by the majority of the denizens of the Eastern Shore of Maryland, it would be well-nigh fatal to such civilization as we have. That is why we Socialists are so eager to raise the cultural level of, not only the Eastern Shore, but of America and the World. It is also true that in a society divided into classes democracy must be tempered by bribery and corruption or perish. We prefer to put an end to the class-divisions that necessitate bribery, sophistry, and intimidation rather than to give up democracy on account of evils that spring not from its nature, but from its incompleteness. Make our democracy industrial as well as political, and corruption, bribery, and sophistry will disappear. That is the way the thing looks to me, and I fear I shall be unable to rid myself of that point of view even if you hurl at me your favorite and somewhat overworked javelin by branding my reasoning as that of a "low-caste man." Incidentally let me remind you that on your own showing there is a large majority of low-caste men in the country and that we still have the simulacrum of democracy, so that it seems entirely possible that the country may yet be ruled by that low-caste reasoning that avers that all men by virtue of their humanity ought to have a chance to lead human lives.

In your last letter you conjure up a bogey and tremble before it like good Doctor Faust before Mephistopheles. You draw a grotesque picture of the emancipated proletariat sending ditch-diggers to Congress. (Do you really think ditchdiggers would be less intelligent *and honest* than some of the millionaires who now adorn the Senate?) "The boss of the union," you tell me, "will aspire to the Presidency. The secretary of the scene-shifters will go to the Court of Saint James."

I feel tempted to drop into slang to express the horror with which this picture thrills my bosom, but I will refrain, and instead inquire how much truth there is in it? For a quarter of a century the working-class Socialists have been sending their chosen representatives to the Parliaments of Germany, France, and Belgium. Have they chosen "low-caste men"? Have they shown what you term the "inherent and ineradicable characteristics of all low-caste men to look with suspicion upon those whose ambitions, ethics, and ideals are more complex than theirs"? The facts are against you, my dear Mencken. No greater orators or abler parliamentarians than Liebknecht, Bebel, and Singer have ever sat in the German Reichstag. Vandervelde is the greatest statesman Belgium has yet produced, and Jaures in France is probably the greatest living orator. These are the men my "low-caste" comrades have freely chosen to represent them. When the Clémenceau Cabinet fell, upon whom did the President of the French Republic call to form a cabinet? Upon that great statesman, Briand, to whom more than to any other one man is due the accomplishment of the separation of Church and State in France; and Briand was originally sent to the French Chamber by the votes of Socialist workingmen.

In the face of these facts you solemnly assure me that your picture "is not fantastic." It is to smile.

In my second letter I essayed the rôle of the prophet, and fell into error by failing to take into account all of the factors in the problem. I predicted "that the present period of depression will last at least seven years unless (1) in the meantime 'the increase of accurate knowledge' or the hard facts of adversity lead us to establish the Cooperative Commonwealth, or (2) unless a great war breaks out." Shortly after I had written that prediction my good friend, Gaylord Wilshire, suggested to me in conversation that the costs of preparation for war might rise so tremendously as to be quite as adequate as actual war in causing business revival. This is precisely what has happened, and we have now started on another great boom. Germany's need for an outlet for her surplus production was fast driving her toward war with England. This caused a great war scare, and the result has been an unprecedented and almost incredible increase in military and more especially naval expenditure. Incredible as it appears the excess of the world's military and naval expenditure in 1909 over that of 1906 is more than equal to what Russia and Japan both spent in the year of the Russo-Japanese War. The exact figures with their sources are given in a leading article in a recent issue of *Wilshire's Magazine*.

I frankly confess my error—an error due to inexcusable ignorance, for I ought to have been keeping track of the increase in military and naval expenditure—and I must now revise my prophecy. We are now launched on as wild an era of inflated prosperity as that of 1905 and 1906 which brought us to the collapse of 1907 and 1908. How long it will last I cannot tell. It is certain that an industrial boom such as we are now having will lead to the introduction of much improved machinery and methods, and thus the more rapid widening of the ever growing gulf between annual product and annual wage-account, and that this must sooner or later lead to a more disastrous crisis than that through which we recently passed. But it is also true that this crisis could be almost indefinitely postponed could we go on indefinitely constantly increasing the stimulus by ever larger military and naval expenditures. Here is the element of uncertainty. How much increased taxation will the ruling classes of Europe and America permit?

These taxes must be paid by the propertied classes, for the propertiless have nothing to pay them with, and in every parliament in Christendom we have recently witnessed the most frantic opposition to the increase in taxation made necessary by the new naval programmes. It appears fairly certain that under representative government it will be impossible to keep the stimulus to business at an adequate pitch. So that it is safe to say that after a somewhat prolonged boom we will have the most disastrous panic the world has ever known, and that the middle classes will be so weakened by the taxation necessary in the meantime that they will be even worse prepared for the next panic than they were for the last one.

As a good Nietzschean this crushing of the middle classes is a most vital matter to you. Where are you going to breed your Immoralists or Supermen after the middle class is annihilated? They cannot come from the gutter. The conditions of working-class life are, I feel sure you will agree, not favorable for their production. Our billionaires may be immoral enough to breed Immoralists, but unfortunately there are not enough of them to answer your purpose. Besides I suspect they have not the right brand of immorality. Where can you find more conventional and orthodox people than John D. Rockefeller and J. Pierpont Morgan? Surely you are not sanguine enough to expect to breed Supermen from such sires?

If your Nietzschean philosophy of aristocracy is to be a workable philosophy, and you have often assured me that therein lay its vast superiority over Socialism, then its workableness is absolutely dependent upon the preservation of the middle class, for from that class alone can you hope to breed the progenitors of your Supermen.

America was formerly the paradise of the middle class. Our typical American ideals are middle class ideals. Our great achievements in history were the work of the middle class. But even to-day it requires a careful search to find here and there a survival of the sturdy middle class who made American history. The railway, the trust, and the department store have either annihilated or transformed beyond recognition that sturdy, admirable class among whom you and I grew up. As independent producers or traders they can only exist to-day by exceeding the rate of exploitation of employees practised by the trust and the department store. They exist economically only by the contemptuous sufferance of their more powerful rivals. Whether they wish it or not the conditions of their economic existence compel them to be either sycophants or vampires or more often both. This is a far cry from the men who elected Jackson and Lincoln to carry out their will at Washington.

Do you think that this change in their character makes them more or less fit to be the ancestors of Supermen?

But the worst is yet to come. Within a decade a new and ominous figure has loomed upon the economic horizon. He as yet has no accepted name, but I will use the name that Professor Veblen has bestowed upon him in his brilliant paper, "On the Nature of Capital." Veblen calls him the Pecuniary Magnate.

The difference between Marx's Capitalist and Veblen's Pecuniary Magnate is this: they are both owners of factories and railways, etc., and accumulate money by taking the surplus-value produced by the workers, but the Pecuniary Magnate is more than a capitalist. Besides the money that he makes as a capitalist (à la Marx) he makes far more tremendous profits as a dealer in capital securities. What he makes as a capitalist comes from the workers and in most cases has no perceptible relation to his business ability. He makes just as much if he is in Europe or confined in an asylum. What he makes on the market as a Pecuniary Magnate comes from the middle class (up to and including the lesser millionaires, and at times including his brother Magnates), and the amount of this profit depends very directly and perceptibly on his ability, or on that of his brokers and lawyers. It is not infrequently to his interest as a Pecuniary Magnate to wreck an industry from which he draws revenue as a capitalist.

Such Pecuniary Magnates as we have yet had, Veblen points out, have spent their years of strength and virility in amassing sufficient capital to make them formidable as Pecuniary Magnates, and by the time the accumulation has reached the requisite dimensions, they have lost the vigor to use this vast power energetically. We have yet to see the power of the typical Pecuniary Magnate wielded by a young man of Napoleonic grasp and energy. But Harriman has given us a hint or two of what we may expect in the not distant future.

From the time that Jay Gould wrecked the Erie up to the time that Harriman wrecked the Chicago and Alton, most of our railway stocks and bonds were fairly safe investments for middle class people. Since the Alton *coup* few investors have been wholly free from insomnia.

Sooner or later there is bound to appear a Pecuniary Magnate who will combine the energy and brutality of a Roosevelt with the Napoleonic grasp and Nietzschean hardness of a Harriman and the sagacity of a Jim Hill. With his advent insomnia will become epidemic in all classes save the working class. Men will seek for safe investments, and they shall not find one.

The feeling of utter insecurity among the lesser millionaires will become wholly unbearable. All intelligent men and women will become Socialists, and the Social Revolution will be accomplished so peaceably that few will know till years afterward that a revolution has taken place.

This is my creed, my philosophy, and it seems to me both workable and inevitable. Given the Napoleonic Pecuniary Magnate, and denying the socialistic *dénoûment*, your philosophy of

Aristocracy seems to me not only unworkable but utterly impossible. Again I ask, where will you breed your Immoralists?

But it is not merely on economics that we differ. Ethically and philosophically we are as far asunder as the poles. I hold that it is profoundly true that "No man lives unto himself alone," and that the most insane sentence that was ever penned is Max Stirner's "Nothing is more to me than myself." I hold that Nietzsche taught an insane philosophy, and that the most logical thing he ever did was to go insane himself. The most sacred thing we know is the individual, but the individual can never reach a high or noble development by trampling upon his infinitely complex obligations to other individuals. The whole cosmos and all that therein is, is dialectically interrelated throughout all time and space. You and I are bound by countless ties to all the men and women, aye, and apes and monkeys and reptiles and fishes, who have lived on the earth before us, and we have just as close and inescapable ties with all those who shall follow us, and with equal firmness are we bound up with all the men and women and beasts and birds and trees and flowers now on earth. Disregard of human solidarity and of cosmical interrelation ends logically in insanity.

The introduction of the Machine Process tended to standardize all life and thus to cramp Individuality just as a Chinawoman's feet are deformed in her shoes. The revolt, the movement to assert individuality, found noble expression in literature. Byron and Shelley and Goethe are full of it. But it was not carried to a false and insane extreme until the middle of the last century by Max Stirner. Nietzsche has done little more than repeat the extravagances of Stirner, though he has clothed them in more poetic beauty in his "Thus Spake Zarathustra." Curiously enough the extreme Individualists always claim Ibsen as one of their prophets. They forget that while he enriched the world with "A Doll's House"—the noblest expression of the right and even the duty of the individual to be herself and live out her own life—he also gave us "Little Eyolf" and "The Lady from the Sea" to complement "A Doll's House" by showing us that happiness was only to be found in love and work for others.

Ibsen should have been safe from the misunderstanding of his teaching that is so wide-spread, for long before he preached his gospel of healthy Individualism in "A Doll's House," he had given us in "Peer Gynt" the deepest, truest, and most delicious satire upon the absurd attempt to "be oneself" at all costs. He had shown that it led to moral instability (if not degeneration) and to mental insanity.

Surely you remember how Peer with his mania for "being himself" was greeted by Professor Begriffenfeldt, the Director of the Mad-house at Cairo, as the Kaiser of the lunatics.

"Kaiser?" says Peer. "Of course!" replies the professor.

PEER.

But the honor's so great, so entirely excessive—

BEGRIFFENFELDT.

Oh, do not let any false modesty sway you
At an hour such as this.

PEER.

But at least give me time—
No, indeed, I'm not fit; I'm completely dumbfounded!

BEGRIFFENFELDT.

A man who has fathomed the Sphinx's meaning,
A man who's himself!

PEER.

Ay, but that's just the rub.
It's true that in everything I am myself;
But here the point is, if I follow your meaning,
To be, so to phrase it, beside oneself.

BEGRIFFENFELDT.

Beside? No, there you are strangely mistaken;
It's here, sir, that one is oneself with a vengeance.
Oneself and nothing whatever besides.
We go, full sail, as our very selves.
Each one shuts himself up in the barrel of self,
In the self-fermentation he dives to the bottom,—
With the self-bung he seals it hermetically,
And seasons the staves in the well of self.
No one has tears for the other's woes;
No one has mind for the other's ideas.
We're our very selves, both in thought and tone,
Ourselves to the spring-board's uttermost verge,—
And so, if a Kaiser's to fill the Throne,
It is clear that you are the very man.

The same philosophy made both Peer Gynt and Friedrich Nietzsche kings of the lunatics.

You will also, no doubt, remember that when the Button-Molder came to fetch Peer's soul and melt it up in the casting-ladle, Peer insisted upon his answering the question:

"What is it, at bottom, this 'being oneself'?"

The Button-Molder's answer was:

"To be oneself is: to slay oneself."

This is the highest word of wisdom of the greatest and sanest

Individualist of modern times, and it is but a paraphrase of the words of Jesus:

> "For whosoever will save his life shall lose it; and whosoever will lose his life for my sake shall find it."

By writing "Peer Gynt" and "Little Eyolf" the author of "A Doll's House" has shown us that he realized as fully as Jesus that love was the only soil upon which true and noble Individuality could flourish.

Marx and Engels expressed the same thought with equal clearness, though with less warmth, in that classic of the Socialist movement, the *Communist Manifesto*, when, in describing the society of the future, they said:

> "In place of the old bourgeois society, with its classes and class antagonisms, we shall have an association, in which the free development of each is the condition for the free development of all."

Solidarity is the condition precedent for the blossoming of individuality. Jesus, Ibsen, Marx, and Engels were all Individualists, but they were sane enough to recognize that Love is the highest and noblest expression of Individuality. Nietzsche and Peer Gynt were blind to this simple truth and they became Princes in Bedlam.

Many a Giotto to-day has no chance to develop his individuality, because he has not the luck to be discovered by a Cimabue. The Socialist aim is not to provide a Cimabue for every Giotto, but to make the conditions of life so equal that no Giotto shall need a Cimabue. We do not hold that every boy and girl has the genius of a Giotto, but we do hold that every human being has an individuality worth developing, and that every stunted, dwarfed, or atrophied individuality makes the world measurably poorer. The present reckless sacrifice of individuality robs life of interest and distinction.

So that, my dear Mencken, it is in the name of Individualism, strange as it may appear to you, that I call upon you once more to become the comrade of

Yours faithfully,
R. R. La M.

MENCKEN'S REPLY TO LA MONTE'S FIFTH LETTER

My Dear La Monte:

Saving only psychical research, no modern cult seems to be so well outfitted with college professors as Socialism. Early in this correspondence, if I remember rightly, you began to set them at my heels—Prof. What's-His-Name, the assassin of the doctrine of inherited traits; Prof. This-and-That, the Austrian statistician, rhapsodist and seventh son of a seventh son, half Diophantus of Alexandria and half Tom Lawson, with his crusade for $5,000 plowboys and a workday of one hour, twenty-two minutes and thirty seconds; and sundry other instructors of 'rah-'rah boys, first and last, specified and anonymous, whiskered and astonishing, cocksure and preposterous. Now, near the end, comes Prof. Veblen, with his discovery of the Pecuniary Magnate, a fantastic and apparently novel beast of prey, gorged to the gullet with bleeding hearts.

The name of Prof. Veblen is familiar; I have encountered his speculations more than once. And his Pecuniary Magnate is no stranger, either, for Col. Henry Watterson, the last of the Jeffersonians, whose compositions I read diligently, has long excoriated him under the style or appellation of the Hell Hound of Plutocracy. Col. Watterson, I believe, is a man of quite respectable antiquity, but his Hell Hound was ancient long before he was born. In medieval Venice they called him Shylock, and there he preyed upon Antonio, the merchant, who preyed, in turn, upon the groundlings of that fair city. Shylock was not a captain of industry, for the Jews, in his time, had not yet invented ready-made clothing. He was, on the contrary, a purely Pecuniary Magnate—a gambler in credits, a fattener upon panics, a star performer at financial inquests and autopsies. Your description of the Magnate of Veblen would have fitted him exactly, as the paper fits the wall.

When Antonio's "argosies with portly sail" were posted as overdue, the gods seemed to smile upon Shylock, for it was out of just such misfortunes that his potency arose. Antonio, the honest ship-owner, who deprecated speculation and tried to put an end to it by lending money, when he had it, without interest, was now in hard case, and had to make terms with the Jew. And, having the advantage, the Jew drove it home. Nothing less than the complete annihilation of his victim would content him. The lust for mere money was transcended and forgotten: the thing that moved him now was a yearning to achieve a staggering and unprecedented *coup*. He wanted to wreck a great merchant, as Jay Gould, years after, was to wreck a great railroad, for thereby it would be proclaimed to all Venice that he, Shylock, was a financial czar of czars. He had the "Napoleonic grasp and energy" of which you speak. He had not only money, but also imagination.

But Shylock came a cropper, and I rather fancy that any Pecuniary Magnate who tries to imitate him in his plan will also imitate him in his failure. The reason for this is not far to seek. It lies in the fact that a Pecuniary Magnate, no matter how enormous his resources and how magnificent his immorality, is still a merely mortal man, whose life, like yours and mine, hangs by a single hair. Cut that hair, and he is no longer worth fearing as an Antichrist, for, as you have yourself pointed out, the might and menace of capital, when all is said and done, are not so much in the capital itself as in the ambition and cunning behind it. Shylock made that discovery when he demanded his pound of flesh. The laws of Venice ordered that he have it, but the laws of Venice, reflecting the public opinion of that republic, ordered also that it be the last entry upon his cashbook. Thus Shylock faced a perfectly simple situation: either he could give up his pound of flesh or he could give up his life. He chose the latter alternative.

Strange as it may seem, I believe that much the same choice will confront the Pecuniary Magnate of the future who essays to achieve the cosmic larcenies of Prof. Veblen's nightmare. He will go on gobbling lesser millionaires until he has sent them all back to work, and then he will proceed to inoculate the middle classes with those insomnia germs you mention, and then he will push up the price of a wheaten loaf to six cents, to eight, to ten, and the price of a can of beer to twenty-five cents, to $1, to $10, to $100— and then, one fine morning, a nickel-tipped bullet, proceeding from a Mauser pistol "in the hands of some party or parties unknown to this jury" will go whistling through his viscera, and he will cease to trouble this harassed world. *Sic semper tyrannis!* Men will triumph over the man!

I see you shudder. You are a philosopher and detest melodrama and bloodshed. You are an agnostic and have none of the demonologist's *flair* for executions and butchery. You believe that the sorrows of the world are to find their surcease, not in assassinations, but in laws. Like the lamented William J. Bryan, and other prophets of the new order, you put your faith in legislation. You propose to abolish castes by an amendment to the Constitution. You propose to perform sanguinary major operations upon the body politic, using one Act of Congress as saw, sponge, and scalpel, and another Act of Congress as anaesthetic.

This sweet faith in whereases and therefore-beit-resolveds, my dear La Monte, seems to me to be as magnificently fatuous as the old faith in divine revelations, holy shrines, and all the other gimcrackery of Christian sorcery. In a large sense, I am convinced, legislation is always an effect rather than a cause, and as such, it can play but a minor role in the reformation of the world. It is inevitably a good distance behind the event, and very often it is shockingly inaccurate in interpreting the event. Witness, for example, the Fifteenth Amendment. Witness, again, the efforts of the Liberal Party in England to overcome, by bills in Parliament, the operation of the law of natural selection in the lower orders. The possession of the franchise did not make the American negro a civilized man, though every one knows that the franchise is an important part of every civilized man's heritage. And by the same token, the state's effort to keep England's loafers and incompetents from starving to death has certainly not transformed them into efficient men, with palpable claims upon life and happiness, though every one knows that efficient men are principally notable for the fact that they never starve to death.

But here I go sky-hooting into the interstellar spaces of political quasi-science when my actual purpose is merely to show that, by virtue of his very mortality, the ultimate Pecuniary Magnate of Prof. Veblen's dreams must ever remain more phantom than actual felon. It is undoubtedly true, I suppose, that men who combine his enormous wealth and his epic immorality will be born into the world in days to come, but that they will ever find it possible to realize their anthropophagous ambitions is more than I am willing to admit. Human existence is not a solo *à capella*, but a battle, and even the under-dog can inflict dangerous wounds. Given certain changes in the time, place, conditions or weapons of the contest and the under-dog, in truth, may suddenly become the upper-dog. I may best explain what I mean, perhaps, by dropping dogs and going back to Pecuniary Magnates. In a struggle for money, let us say, between a Pecuniary Magnate and the great masses of the plain people, it is obvious that the Magnate has enormous advantages, for struggling for money is his profession, and he has not only acquired extraordinary skill in it, but he has also attained to a monopoly of the necessary materials and apparatus. But suppose the efforts of this Magnate are suddenly shifted from the struggle for money to a struggle to remain alive, or to keep out of jail. Has he any advantages now? Not at all. On the contrary, he suffers enormous disadvantages—so enormous that they place him completely at the mercy of his foes. If more than half of them decide, for instance, that he must go to jail for the rest of his life, or that he must pay a half or all of his fortune into the common treasury in expiation of his misdeeds, he must inevitably do these things. Nothing in the world can save him then, for once in jail, his stock market generalship becomes as useless as his automobile, and once his money is gone, it can no longer buy him liberty. Going further, it is demonstrable, I think, that if but one solitary man in all his host of foes decides firmly that he must die for the public good, he will inevitably die on schedule time. And once dead, he is no longer a Pecuniary Magnate.

The easy answer to all this is that the experience of the past and present proves the Magnate to stand in no such perils. There is John D. Rockefeller, for example. Has he been sent to jail? Has anyone tried to kill him, or even advocated killing him? When that $32,000,000 fine was assessed against him did anyone save Judge Landis believe seriously that he would ever have to pay it? As a sincere friend, my dear La Monte, I warn you to steer clear of this easy answer, for lurking beneath it there is a very serious criticism of Socialism, which criticism, I may as well explain at once, lies in the fact that the vast majority of sane persons hold all of your socialistic scarecrows and bugaboos to be harmless. The American people, in a word, permit John D. Rockefeller to live because, after giving a great deal of attention to him and listening to all of the pleas for his extinction, they have decided (that is, through the medium of their regular staff of leaders, bosses, and law-makers) that it would be childish and useless to kill him, or even to send him to jail, or to confiscate his millions. True enough, he makes an excellent profit on the oil he sells, but it is hard to convince a nation of traders that such an accomplishment, in itself, is felonious, or even in bad taste. True enough, he devotes a good deal of money to evangelistic futilities, but what taxpayer, paying policeman and fireman to guard untaxed convents, mosques, and mission houses, will throw the first stone? No; John will never do as a Hell Hound. He is valuable as a herring, to drag across the trail in political campaigns, and he provides a livelihood, as Immoralist, to a few dozen Juniuses of the uplift magazines, but the only permanent emotion that his life and deeds nourish in the breast of the average healthy American is that of envy. There, but for the unfairness of God, go I. So says the ultimate consumer. He envies John, but does not hate him.

Do I hear you say that John is not the worst— that his industrial enterprise and wise spending in some measure mitigate his money-changing—that he is not, at bottom, true to the Pecuniary Magnate type? Shame on you! The spectacle of a good Socialist defending Rockefeller, even with reservations and apologies, is indecent. I shall save you the threatened disgrace by defending him myself. That is to say, I shall concede that Rockefeller is not a fair specimen of the Veblenian Magnate, for his principal business is that of selling oil, and not that of raiding the stock market. Such raiding as he has essayed has been prompted, indeed, chiefly by lawful, and even laudable, notions of self-defense. He is not a speculator and his activities have seldom produced the insomnia of which you speak in the retired shop-keepers, widows, and superannuated clergymen who invest their all in the securities of Mexican mines and other rosy enterprises.

But John's disqualification need not halt us. He fails to meet Prof. Veblen's specifications, but that does not prove the Pecuniary Magnate to be a mere John Doe of the Socialist indictment. This Magnate, you may argue, actually does exist, healthy, happy, and immoral, with his atrophied conscience, his exaggerated ego, and his sneer upon his face. One day we find him cornering the wheat market in Chicago; and next day he is bearing Coppers in New York. In legitimate commerce and industry he has no interest whatever. His business is to sell, at famine prices, commodities that he does not own; to lend at usurious rates money that he doesn't possess; to prey, in a word, upon fear, poverty, hunger, and sore need; to profit inhumanly by droughts, catastrophes, and acts of God. His name, in the wheat pit or on the curb, is Joe Leiter, or Curtis Jadwin, or Charlie Morse. He is as nefariously useless as an archbishop, and as indecently unpatriotic as a politician.

Is there anything to be said for this man? Does any extant system of political economy, ethics, or theology defend him? Does anyone propose a vote of thanks to him for his perilous and painful labors? I think not. Not even the church, which has room on its roll of honor for witch-burners, tyrants, and cut-throats unspeakable, for the savages who killed Bruno and drove Galileo to his knees—not even the church undertakes to clasp this adventurer to its bosom. It will take his money, true enough, and it will even point out to him the prudence of being liberal, but it will not guarantee him safe conduct beyond the Styx. In a word, the whole world is this man's foe—*but only when it sits down calmly, as moralist, to ponder his misdeeds.*

You catch my meaning, of course. It is this: that the world seldom sits down calmly, as moralist, to ponder anything; that the world, as a world, finds any serious meditation a toilsome and feverish business. Its acts, like those of a woman, are the product, not of ratiocination, but of emotion. Now and then, a gust of violent anger strikes it, and then it is for stamping out this Pecuniary Magnate on the instant, as one stamps out a spider, and without paying any regard whatever to the laws it has made in the past, or to the rights that may belong to its victim as criminal. At such times he appears in but one aspect; he is a villain undiluted, a wretch beyond mercy, a felon unpardonable. The fact that he may also bear other aspects—that he may be a freeman and a taxpayer, guaranteed by law in the enjoyment of his property; that he may have a wife or wives and innumerable children depending upon him for support, that he may hold excellent views regarding total immersion, the glory of the Stars and Stripes, and the curse of rum—all of this is forgotten. He appears merely as a captured outlaw, waiting to be lynched, and while the public anger flames, nothing is thought of but the rope.

But the emotion of anger, luckily for all such gentlemen, is short-lived. You and I, for all our self-indulgence and lack of piety, find it impossible to be thoroughly angry for more than the fraction of an hour. Ten minutes after the drum ceases to thunder beneath my window I cease to damn the Salvation Army and the laws which permit it to torture me. Ten minutes after the first spurt of blood you rescue your offending razor from its exile in the ash-barrel. The public sticks to anger longer, but not much longer. By dint of heroic effort, it sometimes manages to remain desperately enraged for a month, but that is the limit of its capacity. Before the chance assassin can summon up his courage, or the slow-moving court can get to No. 2367, or the conservative committee is ready to report H. B. 6667, the public's temperature is back at 98.5, its pulse has sunk to 75, and the reaction has set in. By that time, as a rule, the Pecuniary Magnate has gone broke. His widowed mother, to save him from ignominious toil, must give him alms from her scanty millions.

No; the public's anger doesn't last long, and is seldom very violent while it lasts. Nine times out of ten, indeed, the Pecuniary Magnate doesn't anger it at all. To the farmers whose wheat he doubles in value, he appears in the light of an economic Messiah; and to the consumers whose bread he fills with gases—well, setting aside the Socialists and other connoisseurs of outrage among them, how do these consumers actually regard their oppressor? Do they denounce him as a criminal and demand his banishment? I think not. Do they call upon their representatives to make laws against him, or even to enforce the laws already existing? Seldom. Do they burn him in effigy, sack his palaces, guillotine his morganatic wives, and teach the young to loathe him? I fear they do not. And the reason for their doing not, my dear La Monte, lies in the fact that they are too busy cheering the sport. It is the king of all games, this cornering of the wheat market. It is made brilliant by stroke and counter-stroke, thrust, parry, and surprise. It has the dramatic grip of a colossal melodrama, with a hero twelve feet tall, and as strong as an aurochs. It is better than a battle for the heavy-weight championship, or a minor war. It has suspense, action, climax. It is sport made sublime.

This, I presume to maintain, is the customary attitude of the public toward the Pecuniary Magnate's most ruthless rapines. When it gives serious and thoughtful consideration to him, and attempts to estimate the morality, utility, and ultimate effect of his activity, it is apt, as I have admitted, to advocate his demolition; but it is quite extraordinary, you must grant, for the public, as a public, to undertake any such elaborate meditations. To the common man, reflection is a painful and uninviting business. There is, indeed, some flavor of the sinister about it. Its natural fruit seems to be paradox, predicament, doubt. His inclination is to get his emotional thrill out of the event itself, and to let its inner significance go hang. He has found, by experience, that any inquiry into causes is bound to engender a feeling of discomfort as acute as that which accompanies his Sunday clothes. It is an enterprise as tedious as standing on one leg. What ho! the band brays and the clowns are in the ring! Away to the big show! Who cares?

But the Pecuniary Magnate—what of him? Does all of this prove him harmless? Not at all. It merely proves that, taking one year with another, the great masses of the plain people choose to treat him as if he were so. When he is a Morgan, gobbling trusts by the dozen, and disgorging them again, after absorbing their proteids, as super-trusts and trust-trusts, he is a hero, pure and simple. The drama of it overcomes them; they pass into a state of emotional ecstasy, as at the apotheosis of Little Eva or at Monte Cristo's blood-curdling "One!" If he is a young Chicago gambler, staking his millions upon the price of wheat next month, he becomes a sort of glorified Sharkey, with a flavor, too, of Dr. Cook and the Wright Brothers. Some hold that he will win, and others hold that he will lose, but all hope for a hot fight. If he wins he remains a public character until the next prodigy appears. If he loses, he is mourned for a day as a David foully murdered by an army corps of Goliaths.

So much for the public. But what of your "lesser millionaires," racked by their epidemic of insomnia? Are they equally fascinated by the rattle and the roar, and equally forgetful of morals and balance-sheets? Experience proves that they are not. So long as the performing Magnate observes the rules made and provided, and leaves enough openings for reprisals, their attention is concentrated upon plans for fattening, to-morrow or next day, upon his accumulated winnings. But if he presumes to play unfairly, or to put an end to the game by laying about him with a bludgeon—then his undoing comes swiftly and certainly. Beginning as a stimulating antagonist, he ends as an outlaw, with a posse at his heels. If he is a James J. Hill, he is relieved of his Illinois Central and provided with a few gray hairs. If he is a Charlie Morse, he is railroaded to the Tombs.

I once enjoyed the acquaintance—to my cost, alas!—of a Pecuniary Magnate who flourished in a provincial city. The father of this magnate left him a comfortable fortune, and some more remote ancestor—a pirate, perhaps, or a militant evangelist—left him a powerful thirst for dominion. Outwardly he was a sober, home-loving, god-fearing man of strict chastity and Methodist principles, but within the fires of ambition raged. The result was one of the most fascinating characters imaginable. He had no vices—and no virtues. Profanity made him shudder, and yet in matters of business he was so appallingly ruthless that he made all other persons shudder. Still the man was not merely avaricious, for it was not money, but power, that he craved. He wanted to fix prices, juggle stocks, nominate senators. He yearned for immeasurable might, not only in business, but also in politics and society.

Well, this Pecuniary Magnate began by getting control of a

commodity without which life would be unendurable. The plain people simply had to have it, and in a short while they had to buy it of him. He forced up the price slowly and scientifically. When competition arose he crushed it out. When protests came from the consumer, and sociologists and muck-rakers began to denounce him, he was ready with mazes of statistics in his defense. Meanwhile, he grew rich and eminent. The plain people were angry with him now and then, but taking one day with another, the emotion that he most steadily inspired in them was that of envy. He became a Prominent Citizen. He was turned to for advice when public improvements were planned, or a mayor was to be elected. He was himself pressed to accept high office. The public, in a word, licked his hand.

Having achieved this eminence, he sought to take a step still higher. That is to say, he proposed to reduce the "lesser millionaires" of his city to that same vassalage which the masses had accepted so amicably. No easier said than done. He bought a bank, he began promoting stock companies; he went into the stock market and began to prey upon less astute operators. At the start there was much ill-natured opposition, for the financiers of this city were an old-fashioned lot, and their methods and ideals, like their actual bank accounts, were three or four generations old. But before long, the more ambitious came to the conclusion that it would be better to join the rising Magnate than to fight him. He needed their capital and he let them in. An inspiring journey to the pink clouds of illimitable opulence was announced, and the airship was crowded to the guards. Venerable bankers hung upon the ropes. Brisk young stock-brokers begged to be taken along, if only as ballast. Small investors went as stowaways.

And then, with the journey just begun, the gasbag burst and the airship came tumbling down. With what result? Did the "lesser millionaires" blame it all on fate, as the groundlings had done? Not at all. They began howling for revenge before the first gust of gas was out of their lungs, and by the time they reached the ground they were at the luckless Magnate's throat. It was all against one. They took his bank away from him, they forced some of his other enterprises into bankruptcy, they gave him his first gray hairs. He is to-day but the melancholy shell of a Pecuniary Magnate. No doubt he still dreams his old dreams, and plans epoch-making *coups* for the future; but no one fears him any more. He made the epic mistake of trying to enslave his own kind. Had he confined his efforts to the plain people he might have been a billionaire by now—a billionaire snoozing comfortably in a Senate cloak-room, with a horde of press agents inventing a log-cabin biography for him and whispering aloud that he would make an excellent President.

I confess that I am not prepared to deduce a hard and fast moral from all this. Does the cosmic process prove that the millionaire is necessary, or beneficent? I am sure I don't know. But it does prove, I think, that he is inevitable—at least, at our present stage of progress. He is one of the concrete facts which inevitably arise to visualize world-ideas. He is the incarnation of the dominant concept of mankind to-day, the palpable symbol of the race's current philosophy of life. He is as authentic, I believe, as any other god, past or future. Legislation can injure him no more than papal bulls injured Luther. He will live and flourish until the ideals of humanity are changed—as changed they must be, over and over again, so long as nature knows no standing still, but only progress and retrogression.

Time was when the race of white men had other ideals and yielded to other gods. Once the ideal was an eternity of bliss at the right hand of the Lord Jehovah. At that time the material prizes of the earth seemed paltry, and men were esteemed in proportion to the extent of their renunciation. This was the hey-day of Christianity, for Jesus Christ was then a perfectly comprehensible character, and men actually tried to follow him. Some left homes and families and went to live in caves and on pillars. Others sought to slay the Messiah's enemies, at home and abroad.

Still others had to be content with imitating his humility in the face of outrage and persecution.

At that time, the gods of to-day, had anyone sought to preach them, would have seemed grotesquely obscene. The Pecuniary Magnate, as we know him now, was then well-nigh unthinkable, not only because the laws of the land scourged him with dire penalties and forfeitures, but also because the sacred laws pronounced him anathema for all eternity. If it were true that a rich man could never hope to enter heaven—and few men, in that day, doubted its truth—what invitation could possibly lurk in usury? Heaven was every man's goal, and the man shut out suffered a punishment which no worldly prosperity, however magnificent, could quite make him forget. The Jews, being accomplished sophists, invented excuses for themselves. They could not escape the penalties of the law of the land, but their rabbis found means whereby, despite their usury, they might evade the plain law of heaven. These quibbles gave them such a great advantage over the races surrounding them that they managed to survive the most earnest efforts to stamp them out. That advantage they have never lost. They are still a bit more firm than the rest of us in their grip upon reality.

After the age of faith, there followed an age of military endeavor, brought on by the gradual crowding of western Europe. Then came the discovery of America, and the submergence of the military ideal in commercial ideas. Columbus showed the marks of all three ages. He was at once evangelist, military conqueror, and goldseeker.

To-day we have lost our old faith, and there are no more hemispheres to explore. The whole energy of the race is thus directed toward completing its mastery over the habitable lands it possesses. It seeks to increase its profits from the soil, to improve its devices for exchanging commodities, to organize and systematize the business of living. The effort is one which produces Rockefellers, Havemeyers, and Harrimans as inevitably as it produces airships, canned vegetables, telephones, and antitoxins. These latter-day barons are merely men who are able to do more efficiently than the average man the things that the race, as a race, is trying to do. They are as truly raceheroes, in twentieth century America, as Ulysses was a racehero in military Greece, or Jesus of Nazareth in dreaming, hopeful, down-trodden Judea. They visualize the aspirations of their fellow-men.

That the commercial idea will rule mankind forever I by no means assert. How long it will remain more powerful than all other ideas I don't know, and neither do I know what other idea will take its place. It is constantly conditioned and modified by lesser concepts, any or all of which may one day conquer it. The military idea, for example, often rises to rivalry with it. For a few brief weeks in the summer of 1898, most Americans envied Dewey more than Rockefeller, and thought him a more useful and honorable citizen. Even the old religious idea of sacrifice and *post mortem* reward occasionally has its meager innings. Millionaires, longing for heaven, disgorge their gold. Whole nations, sunk into Christian bathos, pension their doddering inefficients, and encourage the nether swine, with orphan asylum, hospital, and almshouse, to beget copiously and riotously, to the extreme limit of sub-human capacity,

My own private view (the child, I must admit, of a very ardent wish) is that the idea of truthseeking will one day take the place of the idea of money-making. That is to say, I believe that the Huxleys and Behrings of the world will one day loom up, in the eye of the race, as greater heroes than the St. Pauls and Augustines, the William Conquerors and Alexanders, the Rockefellers, Cecil Rhodeses, Krupps, and Morgans. But that day is far distant. As yet there is scarcely a sign of its dawn. The name of Huxley is still as strange, to the common people, as that of Duns Scotus. His influence upon their daily thought is still infinitely remote and infinitesimal. They still pay numbskulls to mount pulpits and preach down at them the dead fallacies of a primeval necromancy. They still insist that Friday is an unlucky day, that blasphemy is a crime, that the Book of Revelation is authentic. The race is yet in its childhood. Its yearning for the truth is yet swallowed up by its yearning for a rock and a refuge.

Meanwhile the commercial idea is doing its best. It is, indeed, a necessary forerunner of that truth ideal I have mentioned. Before we may seek the ultimate verities with any hope of success, we must first put our house in order. We must complete our mastery of those natural forces which will help us, being enchained, just as readily as they now destroy us, being free. We must solve the problems of food-supply, of transportation, of government. We must so organize the business of living that it will adapt itself, constantly and automatically, to the vicissitudes of terrestrial life. At present, if I may be permitted a metaphor, the body politic suffers from stiff knees, a bad stomach, and a disordered mind. It is our present effort to give it clean, red blood, flowing freely—clean, red blood, hard muscles, an alert brain, and a sound digestion.

Would Socialism lend a hand in this gigantic therapy? I think not. It would merely make the cure more difficult. To-day the law of natural selection is aiding the man-made laws of artificial selection. Under Socialism the unfit would survive. Under Socialism the efficient man would have a price upon his head.

Faithfully,
H. L. M.

LA MONTE'S SIXTH LETTER

My Dear Mencken:

I have been highly entertained by your vivacious trituration of the hapless Pecuniary Magnate, though I was greatly surprised that you so magnified his importance as to devote over six thousand words to replying to an argument that I presented in six hundred.

But, before commenting briefly on your argument on this subject, will you permit me to remind you that your promise in your first letter "to draw, bit by bit, once more," your "ideal picture" (of future society) is still unfulfilled? It may be that I am obtuse, but certainly I have no more definite idea of your ideal than I had before this correspondence began. I hope that you will devote your next letter to enlightening me on this point.

I will anticipate your reply that I have given you no definite picture of my own ideal, by reminding you that the Socialist ideal has been so frequently sketched by master hands that I have felt it unnecessary and a waste of space once again to draw it here. But, while it is absurd to attempt to give a detailed description of a future stage of social evolution, and, while no ideal is to be considered ultimate or final, but rather as the starting point for new and indefinite progress, it is still entirely reasonable for the opponents of Socialism to demand some sort of concrete picture of the sort of society Socialists expect to see succeed Capitalism. The picture drawn by William Morris in "News from Nowhere" seems to me so infinitely preferable in every way to the conditions surrounding us, that I, for one, would be delighted to see it realized to-morrow.

But, let me repeat, this is not my ultimate ideal, for I have no ultimate ideal, as I do not expect social evolution to come to a standstill till this old world shall be, in the words of Tennyson, "as dead as yon dead earth, the moon."

Let me guard against a probable misapprehension. By reading "News from Nowhere" you might not unnaturally get the idea that in my ideal society but little use would be made of machinery. On the contrary, as I have said elsewhere, I believe the Machine Age to be still in its infancy. I believe that after the Social Revolution machinery will be so developed that practically all the unattractive and toilsome work of the world will be done by machinery, and that the work that will be left for manual labor will all come under the category of Art, using that word in a broad and true sense.

I believe that this was also not very far from the expectation of William Morris, for, writing of machinery in "Signs of Change," he said:

"In a true society these miracles of ingenuity would be for the first time used for minimizing the amount of time spent in unattractive labor, which by their means might be so reduced as to be but a very light burden on each individual. All the more as these machines would most certainly be very much improved when it was no longer a question as to whether their improvement would 'pay' the individual, but rather whether it would benefit the community."

So much for my ideal; will you give me an equally definite idea of your own?

Now, to return to the Pecuniary Magnate, if I have analyzed your somewhat rambling (pardon me) remarks correctly, they amount in substance to this. You do not deny that sooner or later he is bound to appear; neither do you dispute the economic effects that Prof. Veblen and I have ascribed to him. But you do say, first, if his career proves too devastating, assassination will remove him. This does not meet the question, for his successor will have equal power.

Secondly, and somewhat inconsistently, you say he does not alarm the people, but that on the contrary they admire and envy him, and are consequently unlikely to interfere with him. If this be true, and I will not dispute it here, he will have precisely the annihilating effects upon the middle class (the progenitors of your Supermen) that I predicted.

Thirdly, you say that while the masses admire him and will not impede his mad career, the lesser millionaires will turn and rend him. Did the lesser millionaires enjoy a cannibal orgy with the late Mr. Rogers of Standard Oil and the late Mr. Harriman of the Pacific Roads as victims? Ask. Mr. Lawson of Boston and Mr. Fish of New York.

You imply that Mr. James J. Hill once fell a victim to the direful wrath of the lesser millionaires. I wish you had been more explicit. The obituary notices of Mr. Harriman led me to believe that it was that prince of Pecuniary Magnates, and not the small-fry millionaires, who occasionally defeated the able plans of Mr. Hill. But I stand open to correction on this point.

You also say that Mr. Rockefeller's activities have seldom caused insomnia among investors. Permit me to commend to you the history of Amalgamated Copper.

Finally, you say the Pecuniary Magnates are "truly race-heroes in twentieth century America. They visualize the aspirations of their fellow-men. That the commercial idea will rule mankind forever I by no means assert. How long it will remain more powerful than all other ideas I don't know, and neither do I know what other idea will take its place."

Here, we Socialists have the advantage of you, for we do know, in the language of Friedrich Nietzsche, "how ideals are manufactured on earth." We do know that human ideals are determined by the modes of production and exchange; and, therefore, we know that the commercial ideal of boundless wealth will persist just as long as the means of production and distribution remain private property, and we do know that the Social Revolution, now close at hand, which will transform these into common or collective property will usher in the new and glorious ideal of social service—an ideal that includes your ideal of "truth-seeking," just as it includes the Hellenic ideal of beauty and the Dionysian ideal of joy.

Only by becoming a soldier in the comradehosts, can you hasten the realization of your own ideal. It is because you feel the imperious strength of this inward urge toward Socialism that you argue so desperately against it. I rejoice at this unconscious testimony to the resistless might of the lure of Socialism.

In attempting to cure what you conceive to be my boundless faith in the omnipotence of legislation you tell me that "legislation is always an effect rather than a cause" and that "it is inevitably a good distance behind the event." You are making progress, my dear Mencken, and I venture to hope that it will not be long before you are able to comprehend the meaning of Marx's pregnant statement that "the economic structure of society is the real foundation, on which rise legal and political superstructures and to which correspond definite forms of social consciousness." But, let me remind you that every effect is also a cause, and that while the roots of legislation are to be delved for in the economic soil, legislation also exercises a potent influence upon the course of economic development.

We Socialists do not put our whole faith in legislation. Our eggs are not all in one basket. We want the Cooperative Commonwealth, and we want it soon, and we do not scorn or disdain any weapon that may be of service in the struggle to attain our goal. We regard the ballot as one of our most important weapons; we even think it might be almost our sole weapon if our adversaries would play the game of political democracy fairly. But we are not so naïve as to expect this. Accordingly we shall use every weapon that the evolution of the struggle develops. The recent history of Russia, Sweden, and the Latin countries of Europe has shown that the strike, in its later forms, is capable of rivaling, if not surpassing, the ballot as a means of Social Revolution. We shall certainly use both ballot and strike, and I have no doubt that other and equally powerful weapons will be evolved in the future.

But the ballot has this distinct advantage: by using it we demonstrate our strength, and the mightier the power we show at the ballot-box, the less likely are our opponents to force us to make use of our auxiliary methods. So that it is true that we do lay great stress upon the ballot as a means to Social Revolution. But we are quite sure that after the Social Revolution there will be little room or need for legislation in the sense in which that term is now used.

In the struggle for Socialism, as in all other struggles, the victory must go to the stronger of the contesting parties. From this point of view both the ballot and the strike are crude thermometers for registering our rising strength. When either of these thermometers shows that we possess the superior social force, there will be need, not so much for legislation, as for a parley to arrange the terms of surrender of the Capitalist Class.

For, blink it, as we Americans try to, this struggle in which we are engaged is and must remain a class-struggle until the Social Revolution wipes out class antagonisms forever.

The greatest contribution that America has made to anthropology and sociology was made by the late Lewis H. Morgan of Rochester, New York. Unfortunately, the biography of this transcendent scientific genius is yet unwritten. His more important works were published over thirty years ago by Henry Holt and Company. Chiefest among them stands out "Ancient Society." In this monumental work Morgan through his study of the *gens* and the marriage systems of the Iroquois Indians and the Kanakas of Hawaii for the first time enabled us to understand the social organization of the Greeks of Homeric and pre-Homeric times.

He broadly sketched the development of human institutions through three stages of savagery and three stages of barbarism up to civilization, and thus enabled us to forecast the future. How did he differentiate the divers stages of advance? By the tools that men had invented and employed, and the animals they had domesticated and made subservient to human ends. He demonstrated that these were the most important determining factors of all social institutions. Man makes tools, and the sort of tools that man has made determines what sort of a society man shall live in. Since this great discovery of Morgan's it is possible for us when we know the tools in use at any given era, to draw in broad outline the whole cultural scheme of life of that era, just as Owen could reconstruct the skeleton of an extinct species from a single fossil bone.

Given small hand tools and no motor power, and there inevitably result handicraft production, anthropomorphic religion, and the natural rights philosophy of seventeenth century England and eighteenth century France.

When the technique of production reaches its present titanic development, the very nature of the tools (huge plants that can only be run by vast armies of cooperating men and women) makes the social ownership of those plants necessary and inevitable. "Private property in the instruments of production," says Kautsky, "has its roots in small production. Individual production makes individual ownership necessary. Large production on the contrary denotes *cooperative, social production*. In large production each individual does not work alone, but a large number of workers, a whole commonwealth, work together to produce a whole. Accordingly, the modern instruments of production are extensive and gigantic. With them it is wholly impossible that every single worker should own his own instruments of production.

Once the present stage is reached by large production, it admits but of two systems of ownership:

> "First, private ownership by the individual in the instruments of production used by cooperative labor; that means the existing system of capitalist production, with its train of misery and exploitation as the portion of the workers, idleness and excessive abundance as the portion of the capitalist; and

> "Second, ownership by the workers in the common instruments of production; that means a cooperative system of production, and the extinction of the exploitation of the workers, who become masters of their own products, and who themselves appropriate the surplus of which, under our system, they are deprived by the capitalists.

> *To substitute common for private ownership in the means of production, this it is that the economic development is urging upon us with ever increasing force."*

This substitution, my dear Mencken, is inevitable, and it cannot be much longer deferred. But, as Kautsky says elsewhere, "when the Socialist declares the abolition of private property in the instruments of production to be unavoidable, he does not mean that some fine morning, without their helping themselves, the exploited classes will find the ravens feeding them. The Socialist considers the breakdown of the present social system to be unavoidable, because he knows that the economic evolution inevitably brings on those conditions that will compel the exploited classes to rise against this system of private ownership; that this system multiplies the number and the strength of the exploited, and diminishes the number and strength of the exploiting classes, both of whom are still adhering to it; and that it will finally lead to such unbearable conditions for the masses of the population that they will have no alternative but either to go down in silence, or to overthrow that system of property."

This is what Marx and Engels meant when they wrote in the Communist Manifesto, "What the bourgeoisie therefore produces, above all, are its own grave-diggers. Its fall and the victory of the proletariat are equally inevitable."

Our present ethics and our present jurisprudence are both legacies from the era of handicraft. Under handicraft it seemed wholly right and natural that the laborer who owned his own tools and worked with his own hands should own absolutely his own product. Property rested, as it were, on the right of creation. But to-day the great mass of property has not been created by its owners, but by the labor of others. But we still adhere to the old ethics and jurisprudence begotten by handicraft. "Political economy," said Marx, "confuses on principle two very different kinds of private property, of which one rests on the producer's own labor, the other on the employment of the labor of others. It forgets that the latter not only is the direct antithesis of the former, but absolutely grows on its tomb only."

The economic history of the seventeenth, eighteenth, and nineteenth centuries is simply the story of the divorce of the peasant from the land and the artisan from his tools. This divorce was accomplished with much violence and suffering, but it was absolutely necessary for the development of the highly productive powers of modern industry. When this process neared completion, there began the divorce of the middle class capitalist from his capital—a process that is still rapidly proceeding. "This expropriation," Marx tells us in "Capital," "is accomplished by the action of the immanent laws of capitalistic production itself, by the centralization of capital. One capitalist always kills many." I have dwelt so often upon this tendency of our modern commercial life, and all American business men are so painfully familiar with it, that no more need be said of it here.

Here in America these two processes—the divorce of the worker from the means of production and the divorce of the smaller capitalists from their capital—have proceeded so far that the further development of our productive powers is seriously impeded. The limited purchasing power of the proletarians who have been freed from their petty property compels the pecuniary magnates who control our great industrial trusts to curtail production, while the fear of the crushing competition of the trusts prevents our lesser capitalists from venturing upon new productive enterprises. We are indeed hard up against the day of judgment. We have reached here in America to-day the condition that Marx predicted over forty years ago in these memorable words:

> "The monopoly of capital becomes a fetter upon the mode of production, which has sprung up and flourished along with it, and under it. Centralization of the means of production and socialization of labor at last reach a point where they become incompatible with their capitalist integument. This integument is burst asunder. The knell of capitalist private property sounds. The expropriators are expropriated.

· · · · ·

> "The transformation of scattered private property, arising from individual labor, into capitalist private property is, naturally, a process incomparably more protracted, violent, and difficult than the transformation of capitalistic private property, already practically resting on socialized production, into socialized property. In the former case, we had the expropriation of the mass of the people by a few usurpers; in the latter, we have the expropriation of a few usurpers by the mass of the people."

But besides showing us the tremendous importance of the nature of man's tools, Lewis H. Morgan, in "Ancient Society," also shed a flood of light on the nature of political government. The two distinguishing marks of political government, or the State, as we moderns conceive it, are, first, the power to levy and collect taxes, and, second, the power to make and enforce laws. Morgan showed that among the Iroquois Indians and other primitive societies in which the institution of private property was not developed, while there was a fairly elaborate social organization, the two distinguishing marks of the modern State were utterly lacking. The public power of coercion was only developed after the powers of production were so developed as to enable the worker to produce more than his own subsistence and thus to make it more expedient to enslave the prisoners of war than to kill or eat them, and after the breeding on a large scale of domestic animals had given rise to large private property in flocks and herds.

Political government has its genesis in the division of society into privileged classes and nonprivileged classes. As Deville puts it, "for the security of a social order involving the division of the population into classes, a public power calculated to compel the respect of the nonprivileged is necessary." Political government, in the modern sense, does not exist so long as there are no classes in society; it makes its appearance in a more or less developed form with the emergence of classes and the antagonisms they involve. The product of a definite social order, it will last as long as the conditions that have rendered it inevitable.

"When, in the course of development," says the *Communist Manifesto*, "class distinctions have disappeared, and all production has been concentrated in the hands of a vast association of the whole nation, the public power will lose its political character. Political power, properly so called, is merely the organized power of one class for oppressing another. If the proletariat during its contest with the bourgeoisie is compelled, by the force of circumstances, to organize itself as a class, if, by means of a revolution, it makes itself the ruling class, and, as such, sweeps away by force the old conditions of production, then it will, along with these conditions, have swept away the conditions for the existence of class antagonisms, and of classes generally, and will thereby have abolished its own supremacy as a class.

"In place of the old bourgeois society, with its classes and class antagonisms, we shall have an association, in which the free development of each is the condition for the free development of all."

Since political government is in essence an organ of conservation whose chief function has been to defend economic privilege, it follows that we cannot destroy economic privilege without first capturing the powers of political government. Here you have the key to the political tactics of the Socialist movement. We despise no reform that makes more tolerable the life-conditions of the masses, but we know also that we cannot remove the source of poverty and misery—private ownership of tools and machinery—so long as we leave the powers of political government in the control of the propertied classes. Hence, the immediate goal of the Socialist party in every country is the conquest of political power.

We aim to capture political government that we may compel political government to commit suicide. As I have written elsewhere, "the state is destined, when it becomes the state of the working-class, to remove its own foundation—economic inequality—and thus, to commit suicide." In the words of Friedrich Engels, "the government of persons will be replaced by the administration of things."

I hope I have now made it clear that we urge the workers to vote for Debs, not for the sake of such crumbs of reform as we may attain by immediate legislation (though I repeat we do not despise or spurn such reforms), but because we know the powers of government in the hands of our opponents constitute an insurmountable barrier between us and our goal.

But, I repeat, the fundamental difference between your position and mine is ethical rather than economic. You hold that the individual can reach a high development and happiness by making high individual development and happiness his conscious goals. I hold that the individual man can only reach a high and worthy, a noble, development, not by conscious self-sacrifice (which I agree with you and Nietzsche is morbid and pathological), but by such whole-souled devotion to the welfare of others as leads to forgetfulness of one's own interests.

Socialist ethics, as I conceive them, are well expressed in what W. D. Howells tells us was the lesson Ibsen taught in "Little Eyolf": "that you must not and you cannot be happy except through the welfare of others, and that to seek your bliss outside of this is to sin against reason and righteousness both."

I hold that, even if the goal of Socialism should prove an iridescent dream, it has already enriched the world immeasurably by the nobility of character it has so abundantly brought forth. It is because it leads individuals to forget themselves in their complete devotion to a great cause and a noble ideal, that it is to-day the most vital regen- I erating religious force in the world.

Socialism will abolish poverty and satiety, and make joyousness the dominant note of humanity; it will make it impossible for self-interest to clash with social welfare, and will thus make the Golden Rule work universally and automatically. "May we not expect," asks Kautsky, "that under such conditions a new type of mankind will arise which will be far superior to the highest type which culture has hitherto created? An Over-man (*Uebermensch*), if you will, not as an exception but as a rule, an Over-man compared with his predecessors, but not as opposed to his comrades, a noble man who seeks his satisfaction not by being great among crippled dwarfs, but great among the great, happy among the happy—who does not draw his feeling of strength from the fact that he raises himself upon the bodies of the down-trodden, but because a union with his fellow-workers gives him courage to dare the attainment of the highest tasks."

Awaiting with serene confidence the soon-coming day when I can sign myself "your comrade,"

Yours as ever,
LA MONTE.

MENCKEN'S REPLY TO LA MONTE'S SIXTH LETTER

My Dear La Monte:

In the matter of the Pecuniary Magnate I am well content to leave you in possession of the field. This is not because I think you have disposed of the few modest suggestions I ventured to put forth in my last letter, but because I see no hope of rescuing you from your errors by the ordinary processes of disputation. You Socialists, when you come to discuss the magnates, surplus values, bourgeoisie, and other fantastic fowl in your aviary of horrors, too often borrow a dialectic device from your blood brothers, the Christian Scientists. That is to say, you insist upon using private brands of epistemology and logic, unknown and incomprehensible to mere human beings, in the conduct of your philosophical feuds. Point out to a Christian Scientist that the influence of the mind upon the liver is infinitely less powerful than the influence of the liver upon the mind, and he will bowl you over with the staggering answer that the liver is a mere delusion of the mind. It seems to me entirely impossible for an everyday disputant, handicapped by a reverence for Aristotle, to controvert, or even to denounce such a theory. How are you going to lay hold of it? How are you going to measure or weigh it? It wipes out the whole universe, as you know that universe, and suspends all the laws of evidence, logic, and causation. It leaves you, in a word, gasping in an empty void. The only thing to do is to steal away in silence.

The same fate, I fear, sometimes overtakes the controversialist who engages a Socialist in debate. My own case offers sorry proof of it. In my last letter, for instance, I pointed out that the Pecuniary Magnate's capacity for evil, while boundless in theory, would be ever limited in practice, for not even class legislation could afford him absolute safety from some groaning hero's bullet. This argument, I flattered myself, would give you pause, but I was wrong. In the single paragraph that you take to answer it, you wipe it completely from the record, just as a Christian Scientist, with one shattering denial, wipes out the whole science of physiology. My argument, you maintain, is vain and futile, for it is not an argument at all. Assassination a remedy? Pooh! What's the use? As soon as one Magnate is assassinated, "his successor will have equal power."

Well, let us look into this a bit. Let us suppose a horde of potential Magnates, all eager to feast upon the public. Many of them have the will and many of them have the means, but the combination of will and means is comparatively rare. But by and by, one of them with the will, by dint of toilsome effort, achieves the means also, and in his face we at once behold the lineaments of the true Veblenian monster. He loses no time; he is at the throat of the great masses instanter. A period of barbarous pillage ensues. The price of beer goes up to twenty-five cents a can. The unemployed stalk the earth in tragic misery. Many of them, facing despair, are forced to accept work from their conqueror. Others, more idealistic, starve. Desperate men murder and rob. Children are eaten. Socialism grows popular.... One day a bomb explodes beneath the private train of the Nameless One, and he rolls a thousand feet down the Alleghany Mountains. A month after his funeral, his wealth is divided into two parts. One swells the endowment of a Baptist "university" in Arkansas, and the other goes to his son—a young man whose wildest dream is to be the lover of a prima donna. Thus passeth the means. The will is already moldering in its grave.

But another Magnate springs into the saddle. He is even worse than the first one. He rowels the proletariat mercilessly. The cries of starving children are music to his ears. He delights in human misery, in unmentionable horrors, in unnamable suffering. . . . One day his foreordained bullet reaches him, and he troubles no more.

A third! He has "equal power." . . . So has the bullet that finds him. . . . A fourth! A fifth! A one-hundredth! A five-hundredth! . . . We come to large numbers. Four hundred million Magnates have been slain. The earth is littered with their carcasses. By their wills they have established 5,000,000 Baptist "universities," sent out 50,000,000 missionaries to the heathen, and founded the fortunes of a whole race of show girls, shyster lawyers, head waiters, and alienists. What a fate! What a taste of ashes in the mouth! And yet the four-hundred-million-and-first Magnate, by your astonishing theory of infinite series, is ready and willing to face the same fate and taste the same ashes. That monster who at the moment you introduced him was rare to the point of actual non-existence, is now as common as heresy. Once crafty and selfish beyond expression, he is now willing to face certain death for an idea.

Frankly, my dear La Monte, I do not think that you have disposed of my contention. Unless I am vastly mistaken, a very real fear of death (made real by practical examples) is apt to shake the determination of even the most determined man. And unless I am mistaken again, a public execution, whether official or unofficial, is certain to end the activity of even the most active, and to make his particular form of activity lose its lure for others. The case of General Trepoff may occur to you. General Trepoff, true enough, has a successor in the office of Chief of the Russian Secret Police, but I fancy that even the most rabid Russian patriot will admit that the administration of his successor, while still leaving much to be desired, is measurably less murderous than that of Trepoff himself. If you maintain, in answer, that there is but one Chief of the Secret Police in Russia, while the United States offers pasturage for a large number of Pecuniary Magnates, of varying ambitions and degrees of evil, I need only remind you that in the cemetery of Picpus in Paris you will find the headless skeletons of 1,306 French nobles of the Terror year, who were, also of varying ambitions and degrees of evil. Bullets are cheap to-day. One or ten thousand—what are the odds?

And yet the Terror did not turn France into Paradise. Of course not! No more would Socialism. The French peasants got rid of their feudal masters, and it was good riddance, but new masters appeared next day. The name of the thing was changed, but the thing itself remained. The same phenomenon would be observed if there were a wholesale slaughter of millionaires in the United States tomorrow, followed by a grand inauguration of Socialism. In that case, my dear La Monte, you yourself would become a Magnate. You edit a Socialist paper to-day and write Socialist books, and the high privates and corporals of the Socialist army quite naturally attach a good deal of value to your technical skill and judgment as a virtuoso and connoisseur of economic disgust. In the Socialist state they would still look to you for guidance, for they would still be common men and as such still in need of counselors, leaders, and masters. You would be, we will say, Secretary of the Treasury or Governor of the State of New York—with a presidential bee buzzing in your ears. . . . Let me confess it candidly; the prospect does not please me. Between communism dominated by Robert Rives La Monte and a democracy tempered by John D. Rockefeller I am constrained to choose the latter—not because I hate you, but because a patient and painful inquiry has convinced me that, on the whole, the philosophy lived by John is Safer, saner, and more wholesome for the human race than the philosophy preached by you. . . . The average American, I take it, agrees with me. Maybe that is why a proposal that Rockefeller be assassinated would seem a joke to him—a joke in bad taste, perhaps, but still a harmless one. Do not worry: John is safe. So long as we proletarians can laugh we are an inoffensive lot.

Your other objections in rebuttal, in the matter of Veblen and his Magnates, I must submit to posterity and a just God without further argument, for this correspondence is already o'er-long, and before closing this letter I must try to answer your charge that I have no philosophy of life to offer in place of Socialism. This charge, at least in part, is true enough, for I must confess that I have no infallible formula, like your "materialistic conception of history," to solve all the problems of human existence. Life impresses me, most of all, by its appalling complexity. It is not static but dynamic; not a being, but an eternal becoming. The constant reaction of diversified individuals upon a fluent environment produces a series of phenomena which seems to me, at times, to be beyond all ordering and ticketing. When one attempts to interpret these phenomena, and to reduce them to ordered chains and classes, the result is too often a futile waste of words. Unlike things are given the same name, and their possession of that name in common is taken to be a proof of their identity. Again, the same thing is given two names, x and y, and elaborate equations are built up from them, without anyone noticing the fallacies that fairly bristle in both members. Most of the absurdities of the quack-science of sociology, as it is taught by vapid college professors, and of the quasi-science of political economy, as it is taught by professors, labor leaders, editorial writers, and rhapsodists, arise out of just such errors.

You Socialists often blunder into the trap. In your last letter, for example, you say that, "given small hand tools and no motive power, and there inevitably results handicraft production." On the surface, this seems to be a sound enough generalization, but a moment's inspection will show that its soundness is a mere appearance. What you actually say, in fact, is this: that given hand tools and nothing else, there must inevitably result the use of hand tools. There is just as much intelligibility in that statement, and no more, as you will find in the statement that all one-eyed men must see out of one eye.

But you are not alone in your errors. Others just as gross are made by all other men who seek to reduce the complex and disorderly phenomena of life to rigid rules. I fall into them myself whenever I set pen to paper—as you have noticed full often in these letters of mine—and only the soothing knowledge that I am not alone in my blundering—that even the Huxleys, the Newtons, and the Darwins are sometimes with me—keeps me from abandoning controversy as an art impossible by the very nature of things. Generalizations, indeed, all have their limits—even this one. Apply them often enough, and you will come inevitably upon some disconcerting exception, some radioactive anarchist. The cosmic process is made up of innumerable acts, and the more we examine any of them, the more we become convinced that, in many respects, it is unique. But because philosophy is long and life is short we must assume, even when we can't entirely believe, that they fall into groups and classes, else we could never hope to study them at all. In Prof. James' phrase, we must use short cuts in our reasoning. But we may still take care, in using them, that they are not needlessly short.

And now for the philosophy which I choose to regard as more accurate and more satisfactory than Socialism. You complain that I have failed to state it in my letters, simply and unequivocably, but you must admit that I have given you more than one glimpse of its outlines. These glimpses, I make no doubt, have long ago informed you that it is, in the rough, a square denial of practically all the doctrines and ideals at the bottom of Christianity and Socialism. Whenever and however Christianity and Socialism differ, my vote is for Socialism, and to that extent, perhaps, I may claim membership in your fraternity. Like you, I hold in abhorrence the false promise that "the meek shall inherit the earth"—the one ingredient which effectually separates Christian morality from all other moralities—and like you, I hold that life upon the earth is a very agreeable thing, and that men should concentrate their greatest efforts upon making it more agreeable—a notion which no honest Christian, with his belief in the ineradicable vileness of humanity, and the futility of human effort, can harbor without a feeling of guilt. In all this we are one, but when it comes to the doctrines, which Christianity and Socialism hold in common, we are two. I refer here, of course, to the doctrines that all men are equal "before the Lord," that a man's duty to his brother is greater than his duty to himself, that the hopeless yearnings of a stupid, helpless, and inefficient man are, in some recondite manner, more pleasing to the Master of the universe than the well-ordered, intelligible plans and achievements of an efficient man. I cannot believe these things. It seems to me, indeed, that they are palpably untrue, and that, by reason of their untruth, they are dangerous foes to human progress.

You Socialists, in the very first paragraph of your philosophy, make one of the errors that I have mentioned in a preceding paragraph. That is to say, you give very unlike things the same name, and then assume that they are like. As examples of these unlike things, I can do no better than mention Thomas Henry Huxley and a man whom we may call the Rev. Jasper Johnson. On the surface you will find many points of resemblance between the two. Huxley was a male of the *genus homo*, and so is Johnson; Huxley had five fingers on each hand, and so has Johnson; Huxley expressed his ideas in the English language, and so does Johnson; Huxley was carnivorous and so is Johnson. Reckon up all these points of resemblance and you will find them almost infinite in number. But, reckon up, then, the points of difference between the two men, and you will find them equal to x^n plus a million. In every characteristic, instinct, habit, and quality which serves to differentiate any man from any ape, Huxley was more lavishly endowed, perhaps, than any other individual man that ever lived; but in Johnson these characteristics, instinct, habits, and qualities, when they appear at all, are so faint that it is well-nigh impossible to detect them. Huxley, in a word, was an intellectual colossus; while Johnson, intellectually, scarcely exists at all. The one pushed the clock of progress ahead a hundred years; the other is a foul, ignorant, thieving, superstitious, self-appointed negro preacher of the Black Belt, whose mental life is made up of three ambitions—to eat a whole hog at one meal, to be a white man in heaven, and to meet a white woman, some day, in a lonely wood.

And yet, by the socialistic and Christian philosophies, these men are equal. According to the Christian seers, they will kneel before the throne of God side by side, and spend eternity as brothers. According to the Socialist seers, they are equally fitted to deal with the great problems of society and the state, equally worthy of ease, protection, and leisure, and equally entitled to have the aid of their fellow-men in the achievement of their ambitions.

I am unable, my dear La Monte, to grant this much. It seems to me, indeed, that the man who attempts to prove merely that Huxley and Johnson belong to the same order of living creatures has a staggering task ahead of him. The gap between them, I am convinced, is greater than that between Johnson and the anthropoid apes. Physically, true enough, there is probably only a difference in degree, but mentally there is an abysmal difference in kind. No conceivable course of training, however protracted, could convert Johnson into an imitation of Huxley. The one came into the world with certain inherited traits, certain invaluable forms of congenital efficiency, which the other can never hope to acquire. The one belonged to a caste of men whose value to the human race, and whose consequent right to life, no sane person would venture to deny; the other belongs to a caste whose value is obviously nil, and whose right to life, in consequence, must be proved before it is admitted.

Here, then, I arrive at that doctrine of human rights which seems to me to be most in accord with the inflexible and beneficent laws of nature which rule man in his complex communities just as rigidly as they rule staphylococci in their culture tubes. Of these rights there are two classes—first, those which a man (or a class of men) wrests from his environment by force; and secondly, those which he obtains by an exchange of values. A man is exercising rights of the first class when he kills the wolf that seeks to devour him, or wrings a living directly from the earth; he is exercising a right of the second class when he takes his skill and industry into the open market and sells them for whatever they will bring. If the service that he offers is of small value to his fellow-men, he must be content with a small return for it. And if, perchance, it has *no* value, he must accept *nothing* as his reward. There is, in a word, no irreducible minimum of compensation, due to every man by , virtue of his mere existence as a human being. No man has any right to life, save that which he proves by mastering his environment.

This view of the world and its people is not quite so anthropophagous as my bald statement of it may make it seem. It does not exclude those feelings of pity, charity, and good-will which grow out of habit and association, nor does it exclude that wise foresight which sometimes prompts the strong man to aid the weak man, that the latter, perchance, may shake off his weakness and become a helper instead of a pensioner. But it does exclude that sentimental reverence for the human being, *per se*, which credits him with a long catalogue of gratuitous and complex rights, all grounded upon the ancient theological notion that he is, in some sense, divine. This notion, I believe, is to blame for nine-tenths of the wretchedness in the world to-day. It is to blame for that unhealthy charity which coddles the degenerate, half-human pauper of England, and encourages him, in the name of God, to beget more of his kind; it is to blame for that maudlin theory of liberty which, in the United States, makes the vote of a

Robert Rives La Monte & H. L. Mencken

negro loafer as potent as that of a Charles Eliot or a Thomas Edison; and it is to blame, finally, for that insidious and paralyzing unrest which, as Socialism or what not, is making the inefficient man still more inefficient by convincing him that efficiency is valueless and even criminal. No great eloquence is needed to make a roustabout believe that he is as good a man as the governor of his state, but his belief in that absurdity is no proof of its truth, and in the process of instilling it into his foggy mind you have ruined him as a roustabout.

In order that the human race may go forward, it seems to me desirable that the rewards of extraordinary efficiency should be magnificently alluring, and that the penalties of complete inefficiency should be swift, merciless, and terrible. It is not sufficient that the unusual man be given enough to eat, and a roof to shelter him from the weather, for such things are within the easy reach of practically all men. He must have, in addition, a reward which effectively marks him off from the common man. It is for him to nominate the quality of that reward, and it is for his fellow-men to determine its quantity. If he wants money, let him have money. If he wants power, honor, glory, worship, let him have what he wants. Perhaps that incomparable—but, to the common man, incomprehensible—joy which comes with the consciousness of work well done will suffice him. Perhaps, on the contrary, he will demand, not only riches for himself, but also a guarantee that his children shall be rich for generations. Whatever he desires, he proves title to it by getting it. In the free market of the world he finds his price.

The man of less efficiency makes a less splendid bargain, for the things that he offers for sale have less value. If he is at the bottom of the scale his wares have scarcely any value at all, since they are within the reach of nearly every one. There is no art at which he is appreciably more skilful than any other man. Therefore, he must seek his living at drudgery, at which all men of normal health are equally efficient. Men who desire to escape their share of the world's drudgery, because more agreeable and more profitable work invites their skill, give it over to him. The thing that he offers for sale, in a word, is exactly that elemental functional energy which a draught horse offers for sale, and nothing more; and the price that he gets for it, as Adam Smith showed long ago, is the same price paid to the horse—food and shelter, and nothing more. If he superimposes upon that functional energy the slightest skill, his pay begins to include something beside the bare means of existence, and as his skill increases, his pay inevitably follows it.

It seems to me that this is an admirable arrangement. If I had the power to change it, I should not make the slightest alteration. If I were told off to create a new universe, I should adopt the whole plan bodily. We human beings may well offer our thanks to it for our emergence from the dumb brutes. It has lifted us up in the past, and it will lift us up for all time to come. It stamps out, automatically and certainly, not only the inefficient individual but also the useless class and the weakling race. Its tendency is to accentuate and make more conspicuous all of those traits and forms of skill which best differentiate the human being from all other beings. It offers enormous premiums to the man who can do well the things which all other men can do only badly, or not at all. It reduces to slavery the man who has only the strength of a weak ox to sell. And in its dealings with the countless individuals between this master-man and this slave-man, it determines every man's value, not by his yearnings or his intentions, but by the immediate value of his acts.

Dealing thus with countless individuals, it sets them off, roughly, into castes, but there are no palpable barriers about these castes. A man born into the lowest may die in the highest. A race as generally inefficient as the African may produce an occasional Hannibal or Dumas, and a race at the top of the scale may have its hordes of idiots. In one century, when the general environment of humanity puts a premium upon a certain kind of skill, the race best displaying it may rule the world, and two centuries later, when changes in environment make some other kind of skill more valuable, that same race may sink to practical slavery. The great reward is always to the race, as to the individual, which best masters the present difficulty and meets the present need.

Civilization, growing conscious of the natural castes, erects them into classes, and then seeks to make their prerogatives and disabilities permanent. But this effort, in the long run, inevitably fails. There was a time in the history of the world, for example, when its priest class possessed absolute power over all other classes—power infinitely greater than that wielded by the military class in the middle ages, or by the commercial class to-day. It seemed utterly incredible, at that time, that the priest class would one day become a rabble of scarcely tolerated parasites, and yet that thing has come to pass. The military class, in the same way, has lost its old kingship, and to-day its very existence depends upon the good-will of the commercial class. Perhaps the latter, too, will be dethroned in time. I am sure I don't know. It is even possible that the "producer" class may have its innings. Again, I don't know.

But this I do know: that the plan of Socialism to lift up the "producer" class to sovereignty by an act of human volition is as absurd as the old ecclesiastical plan to solve the riddles of the universe by revelation and anathema. If the thing ever comes to pass at all, it must come by slow stages and as a symptom of changes in the needs and desires of the human race. At present the race seems to stand most in need of improvements in the art of life. To the man who offers it a secret password to heaven, it gives little, for it is little interested in heaven, but for him who offers it some new scheme to attain ease and comfort—some improvement in marketing petroleum, some device for making travel safer, some new food, some new plan of investing savings—it has rewards as large as those that once went to popes and emperors. And in this favored class of services, it esteems most the unique service. To the man who makes shoes which, whatever their excellence, are no more comfortable than the shoes made at the next bench, it gives a comparatively small reward. And so, too, it has no prize for the man who raises wheat in the old, old way, and stores it in his bin. But to the man who, by inventing new machinery or by better organizing the work, improves the comfort of shoes, and to the man who buys the wheat of the farmers and hauls it craftily to where it is most needed—to these men it gives extraordinary rewards.

The effort to lift the man of common service to the level of the man of uncommon service seems to me not only pernicious, but also, in the long run, inevitably futile. When the workingman, going into the market to sell his skill, attempts, by fair means, to strike the best bargain he may, he has my unfeigned sympathy. But when, as a man of common skill, he demands the rewards and consideration due only to the man of uncommon skill, it seems to me that the more efficient men on the other side of the counter are within their rights when they use their power and cunning to oppose his exactions. His notion that in addition to his just wages he deserves a definite reward for the mere act of remaining alive is one to which I cannot subscribe. And his further notion that his mere condition of aliveness makes him as fit to solve the most difficult problems of existence as those men whose extraordinary efficiency has lifted them up—in this matter, too, I must diverge from him. No one, I am sure, regards it as an act of tyranny that bricklayers have no vote in the determination of the treatment of pneumonia. In the same way it seems to me equally natural that negro farm hands should have no voice in the determination of those great questions of government, commerce, and the art of living which sorely tax even the highest men.

But do the great rewards always go to the most efficient and worthy? How about the idle rich. And how about luck and brute strength? Is there any excuse for the besotted master of inherited millions, dragging out his useless days in selfindulgence? And isn't it a fact that the bitter struggle for existence, in destroying a weak body, may also destroy an incomparable mind? And finally, isn't it true that the sole difference between master and slave is sometimes a mere difference in opportunity?

The idle rich first. What of them? Does my scheme of things justify them? To be sure it does not—but neither does it demand their immediate and melodramatic extinction. Admitting them to be as sinister as you Socialists accuse them of being, two factors, it seems to me, tend to dilute their capacity for actual evil-doing. One is the fact that they are few in number, and the other is the fact that their hold upon their opulence is always precarious. In other words, the utterly idle man, who, despite his idleness, retains his riches, is an excessively rare individual. You must go to the stage and the uplift magazines to find him in force. In real life he is met with as seldom as a married philosopher or the horrid behemoth of Holy Writ.

The vast majority of our millionaires are not idle parasites, but simply well-paid workmen. The money that rolls in upon them is their wage for devoting extraordinary talents to extraordinary acts. That these acts are sometimes judged to be immoral by eminent (though self-appointed) experts has nothing to do with the case, for in the struggle for existence an act is never actually moral or immoral, but only (in the broadest sense of the words) profitable or unprofitable, worth doing or not worth doing. The view of it taken by a moralist, however accomplished he may be, is always a mere opinion, and you can always find some other moralist to contradict it. To show you how nearly this is true, I need only recall to you that practically every act possible to human beings has been the storm-center of furious moral debates. To one man the act of eating flesh seems indecent, while to another it appears as the most agreeable operation imaginable. To one man the habit of taking money from ignorant folk, on the promise of getting them into heaven, seems the most dignified and honorable of human avocations, while to me it bears the aspect of a peculiarly heartless and nefarious form of fraud. To one man the soldier is a hero; to another, he is a vile loafer and chronic criminal. To one, marriage is a holy sacrament; to another, it is a dangerous vice. In view of all this, is it for you or me to determine, once and for all time, that the manner in which a particular millionaire makes his money is immoral? I think not. So long as the millionaire himself thinks he earns it honestly, it is probably best to give him the benefit of the doubt. For all I know, even the cornering of the wheat market may have some recondite value; and whether intrinsically valuable or not, it is certainly valued, for the public pays for it lavishly.

No; the average millionaire is no inert leech, but a busy toiler. Even when his wealth comes to him as a free gift from his father, he must work hard to retain it. If you have ever had the care of any amount of capital, however small, you will have to admit that this is true. A further and familiar proof is offered by the fact that great fortunes seldom remain intact for more than a few generations. The rich man can be entirely idle only at enormous expense. It sometimes costs him a million dollars to nurse a bad cold, for while he is *incommunicado* all the rest of humanity joins in a desperate effort to relieve him of his fiscal burdens. The noble families of England, protected in their properties by the most cunning laws ever devised by man, are yet far from secure. According to one painstaking investigator, not more than five per cent. of the great fortunes of that country's peerage have come down unbroken for two generations. Noble and rich clans, as a rule, are quickly absorbed into the proletariat. The great-grandson of a duke may be a barber.

But even admitting the idle and rich son of a millionaire to be entirely and perniciously useless, I fail to see what can be fairly done about it. His father received from the public certain enormous sums for certain services, which, by the law of supply and demand, bore a high market value, and, as I have shown before, they went to him upon the distinct understanding that he was to have the free use of them. If he had chosen to devote them to useful public purposes, no one would have objected; and if he had chosen to pay them, on his deathbed, into the public treasury, even you Socialists would have hailed him as moral. Why should he be denounced, then, because he chose to hand them over to his dissolute and half-imbecile son? Would it be fair or honest, after making a definite treaty with him, to abrogate it without his consent? And would it be even expedient? Isn't it plain enough that his idle son is the worst of all possible foes to impregnable wealth?

And now for the other objections. Do the greatest rewards really go to the most efficient and worthy? Doesn't the struggle for existence, by warring upon weak bodies, sometimes rob the world of incomparable minds? And doesn't luck play the principal part in the struggle? I answered most of these questions, I believe, in a former letter, but it may be well to repeat my general answer here. It is this: that I am concerned in this discussion with the world as it is, and not with the world as it might or should be. If it were possible, by a human act, to nullify the law that the fittest shall survive, Socialism and all other schemes of that sort would become reasonable—I grant only their reasonableness, mind you, and not their truth—but as things stand it seems to me that they are almost beyond the pale of debatable ideas. Whether for woe or weal, nature provides that the strong shall have an advantage over the weak, and that the fortunate shall outrun the luckless in the race. It is scarcely worth while for us to attempt to judge nature here. All we may safely do is to make a note of the fact that this scheme of things, whatever its horrors, at least makes for progress; and to thank whatever gods there be that we, personally, are measurably removed from the bottom of the scale.

I am not a religious man, but I cannot think upon my own good fortune in life without a feeling that my thanks should go forth, somewhere and to someone. Wealth and eminence and power are beyond my poor strength and skill, but on the side of sheer chance I am favored beyond all computation. My day's work is not an affliction, but a pleasure; my labor, selling in the open market, brings me the comforts that I desire; I am assured against all but a remote danger of starvation in my old age. Outside my window, in the street, a man labors in the rain with pick and shovel, and his reward is merely a roof for to-night and tomorrow's three meals. Contemplating the difference between his luck and mine, I cannot fail to wonder at the eternal meaninglessness of life. I wonder thus and pity his lot, and then, after awhile, perhaps, I begin to reflect that in many ways he is probably luckier than I.

But I wouldn't change places with him.

Sincerely,
MENCKEN.

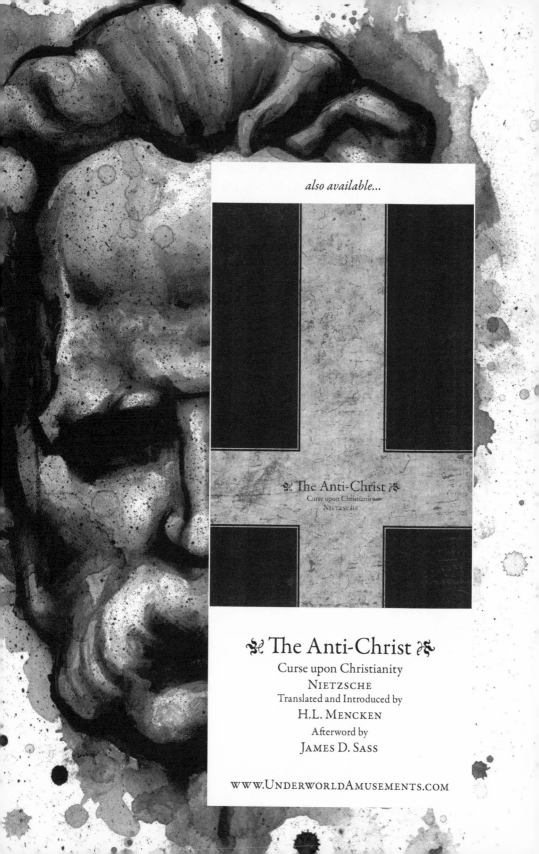

Made in the USA
Lexington, KY
31 December 2011